STUFF MISSED IN HISTORY CLASS

A Guide to History's
Biggest Myths,
Mysteries, and Marvels

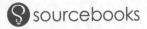

Copyright © 2013, 2014 by HowStuffWorks
Cover and internal design © 2014 by Sourcebooks, Inc.
Cover design by Krista Joy Johnson
Cover images © Sergey Nikolaev/Corbis, Goddard_Photography/
Thinkstock, Martin Child/GettyImages

Sourcebooks and the colophon are registered trademarks of Sourcebooks,
Inc.

This publication is designed to provide accurate and authoritative information in regard to the subject matter covered. It is sold with the
understanding that the publisher is not engaged in rendering legal, ac-
counting, or other professional service. If legal advice or other expert assistance is required, the services of a competent professional person should
be sought.—*From a Declaration of Principles Jointly Adopted by a Committee
of the American Bar Association and a Committee of Publishers and Associations*

All brand names and product names used in this book are trademarks,
registered trademarks, or trade names of their respective holders. Sourcebooks, Inc., is not associated with any product or vendor in this book.

Published by Sourcebooks, Inc.
P.O. Box 4410, Naperville, Illinois 60567-4410
(630) 961-3900
Fax: (630) 961-2168
www.sourcebooks.com

Library of Congress Cataloging-in-Publication Data is on file with the
publisher.

Printed and bound in the United States of America.

VP 10 9 8 7 6 5 4 3 2 1

Contents

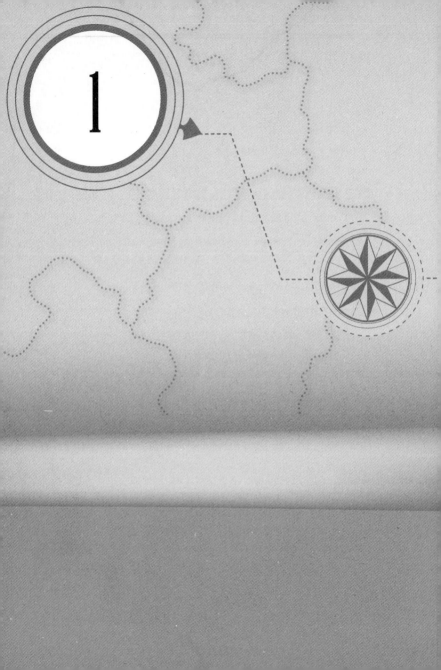

The Real Stuff You
Missed in History Class

Let's face it: we humans are quite impressive. Since the dawn of our species, we have steadily carved our indelible mark on the world. Our rich history is peppered with events and discoveries that are amazing, devastating, and sometimes downright bizarre. Some of these you may have been taught so often in school that you think you could write your own textbook: Shakespeare, the American Civil War, putting a man on the moon, Napoleon, the Silk Road to China. But you might be surprised to discover that much of what you learned in history, in the news, or elsewhere is only half the story. Some common historical knowledge is just plain wrong. And some of the most interesting historical events have never made it onto our radar.

We, the experts at HowStuffWorks, decided it's time to set the historical record straight. We put our heads together to give you a crash course in world history—but not just *any* world history. For this book, we've gathered some of the coolest, funniest, weirdest, and best things that have happened in, well, in *history*. In the following sections, you'll get the real scoop on everything from cave dwellers and ninja to the real Three Musketeers and the biggest bank robberies and art heists pulled off in plain sight. In short, all of the stuff you never learned in history class.

To cram in as much as possible (we want to make sure you get your money's worth after all), we've included sidebars, time lines, fun facts, trivia, and historical notes that will make you the most interesting guy or gal at your next cocktail party. We've also thrown in a couple quizzes here and there—just to make sure you're paying attention, of course.

So without further ado, let's dive in. Where to start? At the beginning, of course!

The Dawn of Humanity: How Cave Dwellers Work

H airy, heavy-browed, dim-witted: this is our vision of a caveman. The stereotypical caveman portrayed in movies and TV shows is a brutish, hulking figure, physically strong but with a feeble intellect, communicating entirely through crude gestures and grunts.

However, anthropological accuracy isn't always a primary goal of Hollywood. In fact, cave people created amazing art, and cave dwelling actually didn't stop with the Neanderthals. So who were the real cave people—and do they still exist today?

Cavemen (along with cave women and cave children) did exist, although perhaps not in the Hollywood mold. Early humans and human-like species used caves for shelter, and the little we know about them comes from what they left behind in those dwellings. Scientists have long debated the role caves played in the development of early humans. We'll never know the full story, but we can piece together a picture of prehistoric cave life through archaeological sites like Lascaux. Within that famous cave in France is a collection of astonishing cave paintings that hint at a symbolic, possibly religious life for those primitive humans.

But early human-like species were not the only cave dwellers. Some caves have been occupied for thousands of years, even into modern times. Some people even choose to live in cave homes today, because they're efficient, sturdy, and environmentally friendly.

What would it be like to live inside a cave? Why would someone choose to inhabit one, and what have archaeologists found preserved inside them? In this section, we're going to explore the pros and cons of cave life and visit the most famous cave dwellings in the world.

THE CAVE-DWELLER ERA

The era that most people think of when they talk about "cavemen" is the Paleolithic Era, sometimes referred to as the Stone Age. (It's actually one part of the Stone Age.) It extends from more than two million years in the past until sometime between 40,000 and 10,000 years ago (depending on who you ask). Ironically, there are probably more humans living permanently in caves today that at any time in human history.

➤ The Real Cavemen

We know that cave people existed, and that early humans and other species closely related to humans inhabited caves. The question is, how important were cave dwellings to these primitive peoples? Because they left no historical records other than a few cave paintings and scattered artifacts, we'll never know the full answer. However, the general consensus among anthropologists and archaeologists is that caves very rarely served as permanent settlements. They may have provided seasonal shelter or been temporary campsites for nomadic groups that moved from place to place, following the herd animals they hunted for food.

Some of the prehuman or human-like species that may have lived in caves include *Homo antecessor, Homo neanderthalensis* (Neanderthals), *Homo erectus,* and *Homo heidelbergensis*. Early humans, *Homo sapiens*, also used caves sporadically. Living as hunter-gatherers, these species didn't create permanent settlements. They had several ways of building shelters for themselves, such as stretching animal hides over bones to make temporary tents, building rough wooden lean-tos, or creating earthen mounds. When they came across a cave suitable for shelter, they used it.

The most common caves in the world are made of limestone, which is eroded by acidic water to sometimes create internal spaces large enough to live in. Although there are millions of caves on the planet, many of them are unsuitable for shelter. The entrances may be located on an inaccessible cliff face, or the entrance itself may be a long vertical shaft. Surrounding terrain often blocks the view of the entrance for casual observers, which is why many previously inhabited caves remained hidden until modern humans rediscovered them.

And it's not just the outside that's intimidating—cave interiors are rarely safe places. They're filled with crevices, unstable gravel slopes, multiple entrances and exits, shafts, and potential rockfalls. Starting about a hundred feet (a few dozen meters) from the entrance, they're also utterly dark. And without naturally occurring ventilation shafts, the air could quickly become unbreathable. A cave suitable for human inhabitants is actually quite rare.

The Neanderthals are one particular species known to have had a predilection for cave living. Because they existed across a wide swath of Europe during a glacial period, the harsh climate forced them to be adaptive, creative survivors. Archaeologists believe they used two main strategies: circulating mobility and radiating mobility.

With circulating mobility, each group of Neanderthals had several temporary camps, some of which included caves, spread throughout a region. They moved from place to place in search of the best hunting grounds.

With radiating mobility, the group had one central camp. Hunting parties headed out from that camp, moving farther and farther afield to find food. In at least several cases, these main camps were caves.

The caves suited the Neanderthals' purposes especially well because they lived in very small groups of about a dozen individuals. Few caves could support a larger population. There is evidence that in at least one case, Neanderthals and early humans lived in the same cave at the same time and shared resources.

CAVE DEFENSE

Caves definitely protected cave dwellers from nasty weather, and probably from a lot of dangerous animals as well. Many animals simply refuse to enter caves, although cave bears would certainly have been a problem. But what about protection from other cave dwellers? That wasn't much of an issue. During the Paleolithic Era, systematic violence was extremely rare. There were conflicts between groups, but cooperation was the norm. Well-hidden caves were probably beneficial, but they didn't need to be forts.

➤ Paleolithic Painting and Other Cave Artifacts

Many of the remnants of Paleolithic societies have been found in caves. That doesn't mean that people spent a lot of time living in caves, but rather that the environment of a cave simply preserved these remnants from erosion, corrosion, and decay, allowing them to last for tens of thousands of years. But not all caves are so helpful. Caves that have water sources inside them, known as active caves, make it difficult to determine what life was like in the past. Floods and changes in the water's course have spread detritus like bones, stone fragments, and tools throughout the cave, often moving them hundreds of feet from where they were first dropped.

Even so-called "cave art" isn't really restricted to caves. Caves preserve the art better, but Stone Age paintings of animals have been found on rocks and cliffs throughout Africa. The most famous cave in the world is Lascaux, near Montignac, France. It was discovered in 1940, and the entrance was later modified to create an entryway and masonry floors for visitors. However, the cave was eventually sealed off and climate-controlled to prevent damage to the paintings, which are very sensitive to the flashes from cameras and the carbon dioxide given off by visitors.

We can only speculate about the purposes of the cave paintings found at Lascaux and other sites. They may have been part of religious rituals, simple representations of life as the cave dwellers experienced it, or superstitious homages created in hopes of a successful hunt. One thing is clear: the main subject on the minds of the cave dwellers was the animal life around them. The overwhelming majority of the images painted onto the cave walls depict animals, most of them herd animals such as bison, horses, and boars.

Some images seem abstract, depicting grid and dot patterns. These may have been primitive forms of calendars or signs, or they may have represented images seen while in a trance. It's just as interesting to consider what wasn't depicted by cave art. The paintings depict very few trees or other vegetation, and few images of humans. We have no idea why the cave dwellers neglected these subjects.

The cave paintings, particularly those at Lascaux, are remarkably detailed. Some of them depict large animals at near life size. The primary pigments used were iron oxides for red and manganese for black. Ochre created a variety of yellow or orange shades. Cave dwellers applied the paint by blowing through a tube or directly from the mouth. They also used brushes made from animal hair or plant material, along with their fingers, rocks, and other tools. Sometimes the images were engraved in addition to being painted. Many of the paintings were made deep within the cave with the aid of torches and lamps. The lamps were pieces of stone with a handle on one end and a hollow carved at the other. A piece of animal fat was placed in the hollow and lit with an ember.

Along with paintings, several other items have been found inside caves that give hints about the lives of the cave dwellers. They made jewelry and engraved small items out of bone or ivory (and probably wood, though none of those survived). Some cave-dweller cultures buried their dead with such items, suggesting some kind of religious belief or belief in an afterlife.

WHAT'S A TROGLODYTE?

"Troglodyte" is a word sometimes used in a general way as a synonym for "caveman." It's a Greek word that, literally translated, means "someone who lives in a hole." There are historical and Biblical references to a tribe of people on the western coast of Africa who lived in caves, called Troglodyti or Troglodytae.

➤ Today's Tarzan: Modern Cave Dwellers

Interestingly, cave dwellers still exist today, and humans use cave dwelling for purposes far beyond simple survival. Some people choose to live in caves today because it's tradition, while for others, it's an economic necessity. There are people who build their own cave homes for environmental reasons. Most modern cave homes were intentionally carved out of the rock, so not many people live in natural caves.

In the Mount Hebron region of the West Bank, in the Middle East, a large clan of Palestinians lives in a network of caves that their grandparents built a hundred years ago. The area has been claimed by Israeli settlers, and the Israeli army has threatened to remove the Palestinians from the caves. While the settlement has had aboveground buildings added to it, it was originally built because the people there didn't have the resources to build houses.

In southern Spain, there's also a long tradition of cave dwellings. Here, the caves were dug out of hard clay and earth. Near Granada, a network of ancient caves is sometimes inhabited by homeless people. Many purpose-built caves have been renovated to include modern security, air conditioning, and electricity, as well as running water. It's something of a trend for Europeans to own a refurbished cave house, either as a vacation home or a permanent residence.

Cappadocia is a region in Turkey known for an elaborate system of cave dwellings. The landscape there is so harsh and rocky and with little plant life that it's often referred to as lunar. The natural caves in the area provided adequate shelter in the absence of other building materials, and the rock was frequently carved into man-made caves as well. In the early years of the Christian religion, anchorites, people who withdrew from society for religious reasons, chose to live there to pray and meditate without the distractions of the outside world.

The caves became even more important in the seventh and eighth centuries, when Arabs persecuted Christians in the region. Cappadocian Christianity literally went underground, building elaborate subterranean churches with arches that mimicked aboveground architecture. These churches grew into an entire underground city. These were eventually abandoned, then later rediscovered by locals who used the rooms for storage.

As previously mentioned, caves are still being created as full homes. A contractor with subterranean building experience can build homes into the sides of hills, dig down into the ground, or convert a previously existing underground installation, such as an abandoned missile silo. An "underground" home can even be built above ground by piling earth around the sides and even on the roof of a house, a practice used for centuries in parts of Europe.

Moisture issues are the main problem with cave houses. Proper drainage and ventilation can help, but an underground home isn't a good idea in an area prone to flooding. Another drawback is light. Living without natural light from windows can be very depressing, and it can even have physiological effects. Cave builders work around this obstacle by using clever light shafts. The insides of the shafts are coated with highly reflective materials, allowing maximum light to travel through them. That way, even rooms that are far from the surface can receive some natural light.

There are several benefits to building underground. For example, the home has a low environmental impact because few construction materials are needed (although care must be taken not to damage the environment when digging out the cave). Cave homes are remarkably energy-efficient. Most underground chambers maintain a temperature in the fifties (Fahrenheit) regardless of the outdoor, aboveground weather. This means only minimal heating is required in the winter, and the chambers stay pleasantly cool in the summer.

An underground home also takes up a small amount of space on the surface, leaving space to plant gardens, attract wildlife, or have a bigger yard. Plus, it's very difficult to break into an underground home since there are no windows to enter through, just one main door and some ventilation shafts.

That said, there are still enough disadvantages—moisture and light issues, separation from society, and space constraints, not to mention a lack of many modern conveniences—that cave dwelling is unlikely to become a serious new trend in permanent housing. Plus, as early cave dwellers showed, and as we'll see in the next section, humans are far too social and eager to explore to stay tied to such small, dark, and damp homes.

THE HORRIFIC TALE OF SAWNEY BEAN

Alexander "Sawney" Bean was reportedly a cave-dwelling cannibal who lived in Scotland sometime in the eighteenth century. He didn't commit his murderous feeding spree alone, either. His wife and forty-five children and grandchildren (most of them the products of incest) inhabited an isolated cave for twenty-five years. They attacked solitary travelers, killed them, and ate them. The depravity ended when the King of Scotland sent a band of armed men to the cave to root out the Beans, who were all executed.

This fantastic tale is almost certainly a myth, as only a handful of reports exist in local publications. No official records have been found that confirm such a family ever existed, and the horrifying nature of the case (not to mention the direct involvement of the king) would surely have left more concrete evidence.

How the Vikings Worked

It is late morning at a monastery on the coast of Ireland. The year is 817. From the shore comes a cry of alarm—dragon boats have appeared on the horizon, approaching quickly with wind filling their sails. A monk runs into the monastery to warn the others. This place holds Christian holy relics, gold, tapestries, jewels, and spices. It is also home to a small herd of cattle and other live-stock, plus two dozen monks and several nuns. All of these things make the monastery a magnet for the men on the dragon boats—the Vikings.

Quickly the monks work to hide the holiest of artifacts and to mount some kind of defense, but the Vikings hit the shore with stunning speed. They wear terrifying masks and helmets of iron, and bear iron swords and wooden shields. Monks and nuns are slaughtered in the attack, and some of them are tortured. Everything of value is loaded into the low-slung dragon boats, including the cattle and the holy relics. The surviving men and women are captured as well. They will be sold as thralls, slaves to their new Scandinavian masters. Anything built of wood is set on fire. By late after-noon, the site of the monastery is silent, the Vikings long gone, and nothing remains but ash.

This is the terror that swept much of Europe in the ninth through eleventh centuries, the Age of Vikings. These are the Vikings as we most commonly know them through the writings of survivors, pop-culture depictions, and even their own epic sagas—brutal, bloodthirsty raiders in horned helmets and dragon boats striking from the northern seas.

But the Vikings did more than just plunder and pillage: they were a key part of a rich Scandinavian culture that not only ravaged the shores of Europe, but settled them as well—often in different headgear than we've been led to believe. Vikings founded Dublin, conquered Normandy, ruled more than half of England, and even discovered and settled in North America centuries before Christopher Columbus was born. They also set up profitable trade routes that reached as far as North Africa.

We're going to strip away the mythology and take a look at the real Vikings and the culture that spawned them. First, we'll try to understand where they came from, what made them so bloodthirsty and what drove them to become one of the world's superpowers at the apex of their era. Then we'll explore the mythology in all its hammer-wielding, horned-helmeted, battle-crying glory.

➤ Who Were the Vikings?

While the term "Viking" is used in a general way to describe the people of Scandinavia during the medieval period, it's really a name for a profession. Calling Scandinavians "Vikings" is like calling all Spanish or French people pirates or bakers. The Scandinavians were also explorers, farmers, fishermen, and merchants—not just Vikings. Indeed, the people who are usually referred to as Vikings were actually made up of several different groups, including the Danes, the Swedes, and the Norwegians, who were themselves often broken into small petty kingdoms.

The actual Vikings were all men. There were no female Viking warriors since Scandinavian society was primarily patriarchal, with men holding most political and economic power. They used their expertise at seamanship and battle to make raids on the towns and churches of neighboring kingdoms. Going on such a raid was known as going *i viking*. These raids were part of an intensely masculine, warlike culture that emphasized battle as a way for a man to prove himself.

The true origin of the word "Viking" is lost to history, but there are many competing theories. Some suggest it's derived from an Old Norse word, *vikingr*, which means "pirate." However, it's likely that *vikingr* originated with the Vikings' victims and was only later adopted by the Vikings themselves. Thus, it may come from the Old English word *wic*, which means "port of trade," referring to the Vikings' habit of attacking such places. Yet another theory suggests that it's based on the Norse word *vik*, meaning "bay" or "body of water," or a similar-sounding word that meant "to turn away" or "to leave on a journey."

In any case, the modern conception of the term "Viking" comes from the written historical records of the time, mostly kept by church officials, who comprised most literate people during that era. Vikings tended to attack churches for their wealth, horrifying Christians especially, because the attacks defiled the sanctity of such places. Consequently, most of the surviving written records come from Christian accounts and depict Vikings in a particularly harsh light. That isn't to say that such a depiction isn't justified—the Viking attacks on European towns and churches were brutal and terrifying—but it only presents one aspect of Scandinavian culture.

WHERE IS SCANDINAVIA?

The region known as Scandinavia consists of Sweden, Norway, Denmark, and Finland. In certain historical eras, Denmark's territory extended much farther into Germany, and cultural similarities are often used to link Iceland and Greenland to the region. The territory was originally settled by Germanic peoples and developed in relative isolation because it remained outside even the most extreme northern boundaries of the Roman Empire.

These people were hardened by the conditions of the region—mountainous, cold, and with little land suitable for successful farming. Surrounded by the sea, they became adept at fishing. Blessed with plentiful forests, they built many boats and developed extraordinary skills at sea. Bog iron could be collected without labor-intensive mining, providing the raw material for armor and weapons.

➣ Giants, Elves, and Dwarves, Oh My! Viking Culture at a Glance

Vikings were pagans—they worshipped a pantheon of multiple gods and goddesses, each representing some aspect of the world as they experienced it. Scandinavians eventually converted to Christianity, but more slowly than other peoples of Europe. There was no central church in any of the Scandinavian kingdoms, nor were any of their religious traditions consistently written down. As a result, Viking religion was highly personalized and varied from one place to another.

Central to their religion were two groups of gods, the Aesir and the Vanir. The gods lived in Asgard, a kingdom that was connected to mortal Earth (known as Midgard) by a rainbow bridge known as Bifrost. The pantheon included Odin, the primary god; Thor, the hammer-wielding god of thunder; and Freyja, the goddess of fertility and beauty. Evil giants, dark elves, and dwarves also played a part in this mythology. The gods were destined to fight against the giants and other evil forces in a battle known as Ragnarok. Norse prophecy predicted that the gods would lose this battle, allowing Asgard, Midgard, and the entire universe to collapse into darkness and chaos.

Warriors who died nobly in battle could end up in Valhalla, a sort of warrior heaven where everyone would get to fight alongside Odin, die, feast, and do it all over again the next day. They were escorted to Valhalla by the Valkyrie, which were sort of like warrior angels who assisted Odin. When a wealthy or powerful Viking died, his body may have been burned on a boat along with many of his possessions, or he may have been entombed in a barrow, a large earthen chamber. In either case, pets and sometimes slaves were sacrificed and buried (or burned) along with the Viking. There is also evidence that Scandinavians offered ritual human sacrifices in religious ceremonies.

Vikings didn't write down their history (except for the

occasional runestone inscription) until they had converted to Christianity. Any history prior to that was passed on through an oral tradition carried on by skalds. Skalds were Scandinavian bards who recited epic poems (called sagas), recounting the deeds of famous Viking kings and lords. These poems could be incredibly long and detailed. Some of the sagas were eventually written down in later eras, but most of them are lost to history.

➤ Beware the Battle Axe: Vikings at War and at Sea

When the Northmen went *i viking*, they were well-armed and armored. Although a variety of weapons were used, including bows, lances, and javelins, Vikings most commonly carried sturdy axes that could be thrown or swung with head-splitting force. The Viking longsword—a sword typically as long as a man's arm—was also common.

For armor, Vikings wore padded leather shirts, sometimes fronted by a breastplate of iron. Wealthier Vikings could afford chain-mail shirts. They wore helmets of iron as well. Some were made of a solid piece hammered into a bowl or cone shape. Others were made of separate pieces riveted to an iron headband and riveted at the seams, or leather was used to connect the pieces. An iron or leather nosepiece extended down to protect the face. In some cases, a more elaborate face guard was built to surround the eyes. Cheek-guard extensions weren't uncommon. Viking shields were made of wood, again often fronted with pieces of iron.

One thing Vikings almost certainly did not wear on their heads was a horned helmet. Such a device would be impractical in battle, with excess weight poorly distributed and the helmet offering no real protective value. Archaeologists found such helmets at Scandinavian settlements and, in the absence of technology that now allows us to date things precisely, assumed they belonged to the Vikings. Such helmets may have been worn by Scandinavian chieftains in the pre-Viking era. The image of the Viking in a horned helmet was cemented in the public imagination when the helmet was used as costuming in operas, the preeminent pop-culture entertainment in the seventeenth and eighteenth centuries.

Along with their weapons, the Vikings are well known for their boats. The Viking longship, with which they are usually associated, was just one type of vessel the Scandinavians built. They made merchant ships and cargo vessels as well. However, all of their designs have several common characteristics:

➤ Riveted wood construction.
➤ Keel (the piece of wood on the bottom of a boat that helps keep it from tipping over).

➤ Single mast with a square wool sail.

➤ Double-sided hull. (Both bow and stern were shaped the same, so the ship could move in either direction without turning around.)

➤ A side rudder.

The hulls were coated with tarred animal fur to seal them against water. In all, a typical 70-foot longship would have required eleven trees, each three feet in diameter, to build, plus a very tall tree to make the keel. Warships were narrower and had more oars to increase speed. The oarsmen didn't have special seats; they just sat on the crossbeams that made up the internal framework of the boat or on trunks that contained their possessions. The oar holes could be covered by wooden disks, and warships had mounts where the Vikings' shields could be lined up, adding extra protection from attacks.

The square Viking sail could be as large as 330 square feet of double-thick wool and was often dyed red or with red stripes to strike fear into their enemies. The Vikings also used metal anchors and primitive navigation devices.

➤ Why Did the Vikings Pillage?

Scandinavians were certainly not the only people of their era to raid and pillage their neighbors, but they did it with greater frequency and a brutal efficiency not seen in other cultures. What drove them to go *i viking*? No one knows for sure, but a combination of several factors likely caused the Vikings' bloodthirsty behavior.

➤ **Terrain**—Scandinavians lived on islands or peninsulas with no room to expand. The land was usually poor for farming or too mountainous to live on, and the climate was very cold. So they looked elsewhere, not only for places to settle or conquer, but also for places from which they could simply take the resources they lacked at home.

➤ **Population pressures**—Scandinavian cultures existed for several hundred years before they developed their reputation as plunderers. What changed? Population. Advances in agricultural technology and the climate allowed them to grow more food and farm more land. The additional resources led to a healthier population, longer life expectancy, and an overall population increase. This population pressure manifested as squabbles among various clans and kingdoms within Scandinavia, but it also manifested as a drive to leave home, explore, and conquer new lands.

➤ **Tradition**—Coastal raiding may have started out as a simple job. Some Scandinavian men made their living doing this dangerous work. But it grew into a tradition that fed on itself, until virtually every male Scandinavian was lining up to join the raids. Young men were expected to test themselves in this manner.

➤ **Exile**—Viking law frequently relied on exile as a penalty for convicted criminals. When convicted criminals were sent off in a longboat by themselves to exile, there was a good chance some coastal pillaging and plundering might occur.

➤ **Greed**—The Vikings wanted things: coins, livestock, thralls, treasures, spices, works of art, and raw materials. They probably didn't want these things any more than other cultures did, and they often acquired them through simple trade. But with their skill at sea and violent tendencies, they often found themselves in a position to take whatever they wanted.

THE FIRST CONQUERORS: VIKINGS SETTLE NORTH AMERICA

Scandinavians settled Iceland early in the Age of Vikings. A Viking named Erik the Red was exiled from Iceland upon his conviction for murder. Hearing tales of land to the west, he set out with a boat full of men and supplies and found Greenland, where a settlement was established. Although the Viking settlements of Greenland didn't exactly thrive, they didn't disappear, either. The next generation would explore even further.

Erik's son Leif, usually called Leif Ericson, headed west from Greenland and found still more land. This area, however, was occupied by natives that the Vikings didn't always get along with. Still, Leif established new colonies and even traded with the natives. But the colonies fell into steady decline after AD 1200, and within a hundred years, both the settlements in Leif's "Vinland" and in Greenland had been abandoned completely. Only oral histories preserved the knowledge that the Vikings had ever visited North America.

It wasn't until the 1960s that a Norwegian, Helge Ingstad, discovered the remains of a series of buildings at L'Anse aux Meadows in Newfoundland. Excavation revealed physical proof that Vikings had settled in North America.

➤ Politics and Plunder

Early Viking raids were launched from settlements in Scandinavia. Following the attacks, the Vikings would return home with their plunder. They eventually began to establish trading outposts in the lands they raided, such as Ireland and England. These outposts also served as launching points for further raids. The Vikings even conquered and held some of the territory they attacked.

In 839, a Danish Viking conquered Ulster in Ireland, established a settlement that would one day become the city of Dublin, and crowned himself king. Over time, the small Viking raiding parties grew into armies. They sailed up rivers or marched over land, striking far inland from the coastal locations they usually attacked. At one point, Vikings even laid siege to Paris and probably would have captured it had the people not paid a ransom.

The Viking army in France caused great problems for the Franks by continually raiding and besieging towns. The Frankish King Charles the Simple eventually made a deal with a Viking leader named Rollo. Under the condition that he convert to Christianity, Rollo was granted the territory now known as Normandy, which in its original form meant something like, "Land of the Northmen." Some Scandinavians settled in the area and gradually blended into the French culture that surrounded them.

Danish Vikings controlled about half of England from the late ninth century into the eleventh century. This area was known as the Danelaw. It wasn't quite a Viking kingdom—rather, Danish laws held sway due to the influence of various

Scandinavian lords. The amount of direct rulership of the Viking leaders over the region varied over the decades.

Meanwhile, Ireland was conquered, retaken, reconquered, and taken again by various Scandinavian factions and Celtic peoples. Eventually, through intermarriage and the adoption of customs and traditions, the Celts in Ireland and the Anglo-Saxons in England absorbed the Nordic people who came to live with (and sometimes rule over) them. These people adopted Christianity readily, though the religion spread more slowly into Scandinavia itself.

In the Viking homelands, governance took the form of a primitive democracy. Each kingdom was divided into districts. Within each district, all free men met at regular intervals in an assembly called a *thing*. Kings, nobles, rich men, warriors, merchants, and farmers all technically had an equal voice in the proceedings, which could include political decisions, land disputes, and criminal trials.

An elected or appointed official known as a law-speaker acted as an impartial judge to guide the meetings. However, those with more wealth and power had more influence than others, and there were few formal procedures. If a dispute could not be settled, they often resorted to duels or torturous trials known as ordeals. In an ordeal, someone might be ordered to walk on water or hold hot iron—think of the Salem witch trials. If the person remained unscathed, he would be considered innocent by virtue of the gods looking out for him.

BERSERKERS

Berserkers were legendary Viking warriors who allowed themselves to be so consumed by battle frenzy that they no longer felt pain. They could strike with a power and fury that terrified anyone who faced them. It is unknown how many real berserkers existed—they show up most frequently in Nordic sagas as powerful foils for the heroic protagonist. The berserker tradition stems from earlier Germanic peoples and often includes supernatural elements. Berserkers often wore wolf or bear pelts and were said literally to transform into such an animal when they fought.

As we've seen, the Vikings wreaked havoc on swaths of Europe, but they also created places and landmarks we still see today. In the next section, we will explore another landmark still standing today—but this one was created to keep people like the Vikings *out*.

The Impenetrable Fortress: How the Great Wall of China Works

L ong before tanks and long-range missiles became available for combat, military forces relied on less technologically advanced mechanisms to protect themselves against invaders. The Great Wall of China was designed to perform the most basic defensive principle of war: keep the good guys in and the bad guys out.

While China's was not the first wall built to serve this purpose (Denmark, Korea, and the Roman Empire all built walls prior), the Great Wall is arguably one of the world's most famous and impressive man-made structures. The name "Great Wall of China" is largely a term bestowed upon the structure by Westerners. In fact, it has traditionally been known to the Chinese as the Wan Li Chang Cheng, which translates to "Long Wall of Ten Thousand Li." (A li is a Chinese unit of length, with two li being equivalent to 1 kilometer.)

So how great is the wall? For centuries, its reported length was widely disputed and considered to range any- where from a paltry 1,500 miles (2,414 kilometers) to 4,163 miles (6,700 kilometers). To settle the debate once and for all, researchers began in 2007 what became a five-year trek to survey the dimensions and route of the wall. This may seem unnecessarily complex, but considering the intense and treacherous topography the Great Wall crosses over— including steep mountains, desert, grasslands, and more— this was no simple feat.

The study, which was being conducted by China's State Administration of Cultural Heritage and State Bureau of Surveying and Mapping, recorded the wall's length from east to west (from the Gobi Desert to the Yellow Sea), since the wall was built to protect against invaders from the north. In 2012, they announced their findings: the Great Wall of China is a whopping 13,170 miles long! That's more than twice the length of the highest previous estimates.

And it was not only the length of the wall that was up for debate. It's also difficult to pinpoint how many cities and provinces are included in the Great Wall's layout. One Chinese tourism bureau states that the wall winds its way across nine cities and provinces: Beijing, Gansu, Hebei, Inner Mongolia, Liaoning, Ningxia, Shaanxi, Shanxi, and Tianjin.

In this section, we'll learn the history behind the Great Wall and find out whether or not it served its purpose well and how it eventually became obsolete. We'll also take a look at the current state of the structure and how it's being protected after years of abuse by both Mother Nature and humans alike. But first, who built the wall?

➤ The Rise of the Great Wall

When the first portions of what would eventually become the Great Wall were built, they weren't part of a large master plan to block off China from the north. Instead, beginning anywhere from the seventh century BC to the fifth century BC (the start date is disputed by archaeologists), many small walls were erected by the six different states that would eventually become China as we know it. The point of the walls was to provide protection from the often warring states as well as a variety of invaders, including the Huns.

In 220 BC, the Qin Dynasty unified the Qin state with the six other warring states (Han, Wei, Chu, Yan, Zhao, and Qi, in that order). The emperor Qin Shi Huang then ordered the separate sections of the Great Wall in the northern states to be connected. He did this to provide maximum security from the troublesome Huns. With that, the Great Wall began to take shape in its most infantile form.

Construction on the wall—which is made of several different materials including bricks, stone, grass, rock and earth—continued over subsequent centuries and was completed by Chinese soldiers, criminals, and commoners. This imposing structure didn't come without a price, however.

It's estimated that thousands upon thousands of Chinese workers died building the Great Wall, and many of them were buried inside the wall itself.

In addition to the Qin Dynasty, other dynasties were involved in the Great Wall's long and complex construction history.

➤ The Western Han Dynasty, which ruled from 206 BC to AD 24, restored the Qin Wall and ordered multiple extensions of the wall, including three sections of the Hexi Great Wall.

➤ The Northern Wei Dynasty (386–534) continued the wall's expansion, adding more than 620 miles (997 kilometers) to the structure.

➤ Despite being short on time, the Northern Qi Dynasty (550–577), added the Wall of Northern Qi, which covered hundreds of miles in many different countries and provinces.

➤ The Jin Dynasty (265–420), the Sui Dynasty (581–608), and the Liao Dynasty (916–1125) all continued the tradition, adding thousands of miles among them to the wall's length.

Under the Ming Dynasty, the wall underwent its biggest transformation.

WHY WERE THE HUNS SO FEARED?

The Huns probably weren't the kind of people who were invited over for tea very often. Clearly, they were a fearsome bunch, given that the Chinese saw fit to erect early portions of the Great Wall to prevent the Huns from invading. Considered barbarians by many, the Huns (known by the Chinese as the Hsiung-nu) terrorized Asia and Europe. Under the leadership of the notorious Attila the Hun, the Huns wreaked havoc on the Roman Empire during the fourth and fifth centuries.

Historians believe the Huns were originally a nomadic group from Asia, and accounts describe them as being fierce and skilled military geniuses and remarkable horsemen. The Hun reign of terror faded quickly following Attila's death in 454, when much of the remaining army disbanded and joined other forces.

➤ The Great Wall Under the Ming Dynasty

It wasn't until the rise of the Ming Dynasty in 1368 that the Great Wall of China as we know it today was brought to fruition. The Ming Dynasty had to contend with a massive number of attacks by minority tribes, so it made substantial additions to the wall.

The complexity and sheer size of the Ming wall outdid all of its predecessors. Not only did the dynasty add length, but it also added double and triple walls in some places to reinforce previously built structures and confuse attackers. In fact, in many places the wall is wide enough on top for someone to drive a car on it, averaging an impressive 22 feet (6.7 meters).

CAN YOU SEE THE GREAT WALL OF CHINA FROM OUTER SPACE?

Although the wall sports an impressive girth, it's not particularly visible from outer space as the old myth claims. If that were true, major highways would also be visible, since many are much larger than the Great Wall. Only certain sections, such as the one in northern China, are slightly more discernible from up above.

In photos of the Northern Shanxi Province in China from space, the Great Wall is barely visible as a black line running diagonally through the land.

The Ming Dynasty also increased the military prowess around the wall. Fortresses were placed intermittently along the length of the wall to store military supplies, and beacons were built to provide much-needed light. Another innovation to the wall that the Ming Dynasty introduced was guards. Guard towers were erected at strategic points along the wall from which guards would send out smoke signals and fire cannons to notify each other of possible hostile attacks. The only major downfall to these guard towers is that they were manned by humans, who sometimes fell prey to enemies' bribes and allowed them access to the other side of the wall.

Construction on the Great Wall was an ongoing and successful effort under the Ming Dynasty until the seventeenth century when China could no longer thwart the efforts of the Manchu, invaders from Manchuria who successfully infiltrated China. This takeover, which brought down the Ming Dynasty and gave rise to the Qing Dynasty, effectively halted the Great Wall's development, which spanned more than a whopping two thousand years.

In the next section, we'll take a look at how the wall fell into disrepair.

LEGENDS OF THE GREAT WALL

As with most ancient monuments, legends abound about the Great Wall of China. One of the most famous and well-known legends tells the story of a woman named

Meng Jiangnu, whose husband forcibly was sent to build part of the Great Wall during the Qin Dynasty (221–206 BC). After some time apart with no word from her beloved, she set out to find him, discovering too late that he had died. Legend has it that her loud, bitter weeping caused part of the Great Wall to collapse. Although this legend probably isn't true, it certainly speaks to the fact that many thousands of lives were lost during the Great Wall's two thousand years of construction.

➤ A Downward Spiral

The Great Wall's downward spiral began when Manchurians invaded China.

The Great Wall isn't just one of the world's most famous landmarks. It's also the only historical monument marked on world maps by cartographers. Understandably, it is a magnet for tourism, with more than ten million people visiting it each year. While its status as a bona fide tourist attraction results in valuable revenue, tourism and other factors have taken a massive toll on the wall's structural and aesthetic integrity.

It's important to note that the Great Wall hasn't exactly been in top-notch condition for some time. Following the Manchu invasion in the 1700s, it was largely abandoned as a military priority. After all, why would the Manchu waste time and energy on something that failed to keep them out? The wall became overgrown by vegetation and began to deteriorate as a result of earthquakes and exposure to snow, wind, and rain. Battles ranging from tiffs with the Huns to high-powered assaults by Japan in the 1930s and 1940s also hastened the wall's decline.

Even local residents' everyday activities have contributed substantially to the Great Wall's deterioration. Herding animals and gathering firewood have sped up the process after years of abuse. Stomping livestock and human tools have chipped away at the wall's edifice. What's more, Mao Zedong holds some responsibility for the damage. He encouraged the Chinese people to use bricks and other parts of the wall to build homes and other structures as recently as the 1950s. Road construction crews have even dared to knock holes in portions of the wall to build highways.

Ironically, the tourism industry is one of the largest contributing factors to the wall's demise. For years, tourists have taken pieces and bricks from the wall as souvenirs. They've etched names and epithets into the wall, and vendors have set up shop with souvenir stores, cable cars, parking lots, fast-food restaurants, and more within feet of the landmark.

Unsightly advertisements, signs, and public utilities have shown up in high-traffic areas along the wall, and litter and graffiti have marred it and surrounding areas. Well–meaning tourists and locals have taken it upon themselves to restore portions of the wall in unauthentic and unreliable ways. As a result of all of these factors, a whopping 50 percent of the Great Wall has disappeared entirely, with a remaining 30 percent in ruins and a mere 20 percent classified as being in "reasonable" condition.

A MODERN WONDER

The Great Wall was recognized and immortalized in 2007 as one of the modern-day seven wonders of the world. The worldwide contest was implemented by the New7Wonders Foundation, an organization dedicated to increasing awareness about the world's natural and man-made structures. More than 100 million votes were cast worldwide via telephone and the Internet. The contest results weren't endorsed or publicized by Chinese heritage officials, despite the results' likely impact on tourism.

Other inductees to the illustrious new list were the Colosseum (Rome), Taj Mahal (India), Statue of Christ Redeemer (Brazil), Chichén Itzá pyramid (Mexico), Machu Picchu (Peru), and Petra (Jordan). The original seven wonders are thought to have been designated by a Greek author in ancient times.

➤ Revitalizing the Great Wall

Until recently, the Chinese government was reticent to discourage or limit tourist access to the Great Wall for fear
that would decrease revenue to the area. However, as it
has become increasingly clear that the wall is in peril, the
government—with input from organizations such as the
International Friends of the Great Wall and the Great Wall
Society of China—has put laws and regulations in place to
stop the damage and properly restore the structure. In fact,
the World Monuments Fund added the Great Wall to its list
of the World's 100 Most Endangered Sites.

In 2003, the Beijing Administrative Bureau of Cultural
Relics enacted regulations to protect the Beijing portion of
the wall, which shoulders some five to six million tourists
each year. The regulation allows the organization the authority to prohibit the construction of any building within 1,640
feet (500 meters) of the wall that can cause either unpleasant
aesthetic damage or physical desecration. Seemingly innocent activities that have an adverse effect on the wall have
been declared taboo. These activities include pitching a tent,
gathering firewood, herding animals, and setting up stands to
charge admission to less savvy tourists.

Soon after the Beijing regulations were put in place, the
Chinese government enacted the first national law aimed
at protecting the Great Wall. The government officially

prohibited activities like removing bricks or stones from the wall, holding raves or parties on top of it, carving words into the wall, or building a home too close to it. Raves and driving and carving on the wall have become such big problems in recent years that in 2006, the government instituted fines of up to $62,500 for institutions and $6,250 for individual violators.

In addition to enacting laws designed to protect the Great Wall from further damage, the Chinese government has also allocated funds to allow for continued preservation and restoration of the monument. Advocates encourage individuals to contribute to these efforts in several ways, such as by planting trees, removing litter, and making sure to never take anything from the wall or leave anything behind.

Thanks to these efforts, awareness about the Great Wall's status as a historical landmark of intrinsic value and beauty to China and the world has become more established, effectively beginning to turn the tide of centuries of neglect and abuse. Unfortunately, in many of the less metropolitan areas where the wall is located, locals don't understand the cultural significance of the structure. In fact, they continue to routinely use bricks for building purposes. Several men in Inner Mongolia were even accused of damaging the wall by removing what they deemed to be a pile of earth from a particularly ancient portion of the wall to use as landfill. Simply put, many people who are just trying to survive aren't as concerned with a landmark as they are with taking care of their families.

Although it may continue to be an uphill battle for some time, the Great Wall's preservation has been embraced as a matter of the utmost cultural and historical importance, especially because it serves as a gateway into China's storied and colorful history.

Top Five Ancient Chinese Inventions

We take a lot of things for granted in the modern world. Fiber-optic cables deliver enormous amounts of information at nearly the speed of light. You can hop into your car and shout your destination at your GPS navigation system, and a digitized and disembodied voice issues easy-to-follow directions. We have it pretty sweet here in the twenty-first century.

As time marches on, it becomes easier to overlook the contributions of those who came before us. Perhaps no other ancient culture has contributed more to this advancement of human progress than the Chinese. Here are five of the greatest inventions of the ancient nation, in no particular order.

1. Gunpowder

Legend has it that gunpowder was accidentally discovered by Chinese alchemists looking for a concoction that would create immortality in humans. Ironically, what these ancient chemists stumbled upon was an invention that could easily take human life.

Early gunpowder was made of a mixture of potassium nitrate (saltpeter), charcoal, and sulfur, and it was first described in 1044 in the *Collection of the Most Important Military Techniques*, compiled by Zeng Goliang. The discovery of gunpowder is assumed to have occurred sometime earlier, since Zeng describes three different gunpowder mixtures and the Chinese used it for signal flares and fireworks before appropriating it for military use in rudimentary grenades.

Over time, they had realized that metals added to the mixture created brilliant colors in gunpowder explosions and—ka-boom!—modern fireworks displays were born. Gunpowder also makes a handy explosive for projectiles like bullets.

2. The Compass

Where would we be without the compass? Well, lost. Those of us who hike in the woods or fly various aircraft have the Chinese to thank for guiding us home safely.

Originally, the Chinese created their compasses to point to true south. This was because they considered south, not north, their cardinal direction. The earliest compasses were created in the fourth century BC and were made of lodestone.

The mere existence of lodestone is the result of a bit of luck. Lodestone is a type of magnetite (a magnetic iron ore) that becomes highly magnetized when struck by lightning. The result is a mineral that's magnetized toward both the north and south poles. We're not certain precisely who came up with the clever idea of discerning direction using lodestone, but archaeological evidence shows the Chinese fashioned ladles that balanced on a divining board. The ladles would point the direction to inner harmony for ancient Chinese soothsayers.

➤ 3. Pasta?

Anybody who loves a good bowl of *pasta e fagioli* or linguine and clams may want to tip his hat to the ancient Chinese for coming up with pasta—not the Italians, as you may have suspected.

The jury is still out on this one, but it looks like the Chinese beat either the Italians or the Arabs (it's unclear which) by around two thousand years. In 2006, archaeologists excavating a two-thousand-year-old settlement at Lajia in the Qinghai Province near the Tibetan border uncovered an overturned bowl of stringy noodles buried beneath ten feet of earth.

The newly discovered pasta may be the world's oldest. It's made from two types of millet grain, both of which have been cultivated in China for about seven thousand years. What's more, the Chinese still use these grains to make pasta to this day.

➤ 4. Alcohol

You can thank the Chinese for ethanol and isopropyl alcohol—not to mention beer, wine, and liquor. Few of man's ingenuities have delivered as much joy and sorrow as alcohol.

For many years, alcohol fermentation was assumed to have grown out of other similar processes. By the early third century BC, the Chinese had figured out how to refine food products like vinegar and soy sauce using the techniques of fermentation and distillation. Alcoholic spirits would soon follow.

Recent archaeological discoveries have pushed the date for Chinese fermentation and the creation of alcohol much further back. Nine-thousand-year-old pottery shards uncovered in Henan province show traces of alcohol. This discovery proves that the Chinese were the first to make alcohol, since the previous title holders, the ancient Arabs, didn't come up with alcoholic drinks until one thousand years later.

➤ 5. Kites and Hang Gliders

Two ancient Chinese men share the credit for coming up with one of China's biggest claims to fame. During the fourth century BC, Gongshu Ban and Mo Di, a patron of the arts and a philosopher, respectively, constructed bird-shaped kites that dipped and dove in the wind. The pair's novelty caught on quickly.

Over time, the Chinese adapted and added to the initial kite's design and found new uses for it beyond amusement. Kites became an easy way to fish without a boat, simply by draping a line and hook from the kite and then dangling it into an inaccessible body of water. Kites also became instrumental in military applications, serving as unmanned drones that delivered payloads of gunpowder to enemy fortifications. In 1232, the Chinese employed kites to drop propaganda leaflets over a Mongol prisoner-of-war encampment, urging the captured Chinese there to rebel and eventually overtake their captors.

Soon, the urge to fly would be married with the technology of the kite to produce another Chinese invention, the hang glider. By the end of the sixth century AD, the Chinese had managed to build kites large and aerodynamic enough to sustain the weight of an average-sized man. It was only a matter of time before someone decided to simply remove the kite strings and see what happened.

The Chinese began using the untethered kites that we know today as hang gliders. However, these "kites" weren't used for thrill rides: emperors found joy in forcing convicted criminals and captured enemies to jump off cliffs while strapped into the gliders. One poor man flew two miles before he landed safely. With these early flights, the Chinese had beaten European ingenuity by 1,335 years.

In the next section, we'll learn about another type of people who purportedly could fly—without the help of any winged apparatus.

The Assassin's Creed:
How Ninja Work

Secretive and silent, the ninja stalks through Japanese history like a shadow, striking fear into the hearts of peasants and emperors alike. Today, the ninja has become a legendary, cult-like figure, showing up in computer games and children's cartoons, as well as an entire genre of martial-arts action films.

But who were the real ninja? Where did they come from, and what purpose did they serve? Let's peer into the murky shadows of ninja history, separate fact from fiction, and examine the weapons and skills that made ninja some of the most fearsome assassins in the world.

➤ I Spy: The Origins of Espionage

Although ninja were almost always Japanese, the roots of the ninja philosophy lie in China, where Sun Tzu wrote *The Art of War* in the fourth or fifth century BC *The Art of War* is a guide for military commanders that is still considered essential reading for modern military officers, as well as businesspeople.

One part of the text, in particular, caused changes in the philosophy of Japanese warriors that would eventually lead to the ideology of the ninja. Chapter 13 describes the advantages that can be gained by spreading disinformation among your enemies and sowing confusion in their ranks through deception and sabotage. It also recommends that generals find out as much as possible about their enemy by using spies and other practical methods.

Much of this was antithetical to the Japanese way of waging war. For centuries, armies of foot soldiers and samurai would line up and call each other out to do honorable, one-on-one battle. The underhanded tactics espoused by Sun Tzu went against the grain. But the wisdom of using deception and espionage to win wars could not be denied, and many Japanese warriors came to grudgingly accept that philosophy.

That said, the mixed feelings that the Japanese had about the deceptive ways of the ninja, combined with the ninja's inherent secretiveness, make studying the history of these shadowy warriors difficult. In many cases, Japanese historians simply left all mention of ninja out of historical documents. If they were mentioned, ninja were either elevated to the status of terrifying, supernatural beings or spoken of with contempt and disgust.

➤ The First James Bonds

The Japanese legend of Prince Yamato is often considered the first ninja story, although Yamato did not adopt the black costume or stealthy tactics so often associated with ninja. Instead, he used deception, dressing as a woman to attract two barbarian chieftains. When the chieftains had been lulled into a false sense of security, Yamato drew a hidden sword and killed them both. His use of a disguise is a hallmark of ninja tactics, so Yamato is sometimes called "The First Ninja."

Another important part of ninja folklore is the story of thirteen-year-old Kumawaka. Kumawaka had traveled far to visit his dying father, but the monk who held the father as a prisoner would not allow the two to meet. Kumawaka's father died before Kumawaka had a chance to see him, so the boy vowed revenge upon the monk.

The teen wasn't strong enough to simply fight the monk and his family. Instead, he faked an illness so they would take him into their home. There, he would sneak around at night, finding out where everyone slept and when the guards patrolled. One night, he snuck into the monk's room. The monk slept with a lamp burning, so the boy opened a window and allowed moths to enter the room. They flocked to the light of the lamp and completely covered it, leaving the room in darkness. Then, Kumawaka stole the monk's sword and murdered him in his bed.

Fleeing out a window, the boy was chased by guards until he reached a river. He cleverly climbed to the top of a bamboo plant near the river, leaned until the flexible bamboo stalk bent out across the water, and then jumped off and escaped the guards.

Although Kumawaka was only thirteen and didn't call himself a ninja, his use of deception, stealth, and cleverness inspired generations of Japanese warriors who did adopt the name "ninja."

➤ Birthplace of the Ninja

The regions of Iga and Koga in Japan are considered by many to be the birthplace of the ninja as a major force in Japanese warfare. The men who belonged to the clans that ruled the area hired themselves out as mercenaries, fighting for whichever *daimyo*, or lord, paid them the most. The Iga and Koga ninja often worked for daimyo that they had been hired to attack just a few years earlier. This reputation as disloyal mercenaries became a trademark of the ninja, running in direct opposition to the Bushido code of the utterly loyal samurai.

The Iga ninja had another reputation, however—one that ensured their continued use in Japan's feudal wars. They were known as experts at infiltrating castles. With their stealthy skills, they could obtain secret information, sabotage enemy supplies, or steal food and weapons. These skills were passed from father to son. For generations, warring daimyo knew that the best ninja in Japan could be hired in Iga and Koga.

PAPER LANTERNS

The Iga ninja didn't always have to sneak into enemy castles. Sometimes they walked right through the front gates. To get into one castle, a group of ninja stole a paper lantern bearing the badge of the enemy daimyo. They then made replicas of the lanterns and marched straight into the castle bearing their fake lantern badges. After setting the castle on fire, they quickly escaped. The damage they dealt was twofold: in addition to the fire, the daimyo thought traitors within the castle had caused the damage, spreading confusion and paranoia in the enemy ranks.

➤ Samurai by Day, Ninja by Night

Although the ninja from Iga and Koga were espionage mercenaries, in other parts of Japan the ninja took on other roles. Many daimyo had elite groups of ninja who were as loyal as any samurai. They served as spies, scouts, or commando groups that made guerilla attacks on enemy castles and encampments. When an army retreated from the field of battle, ninja with firearms were left lying in hiding to attack the oncoming enemy soldiers.

Ninja were particularly useful when a castle was under siege. In such circumstances, the ninja were often the only people who could sneak out of the castle. In one case, a ninja left the castle at night, entered the enemy camp, and stole their flag. The next morning, the enemy's army awoke to find their own flag waving mockingly in the breeze from the castle wall. The moral victory accomplished by humiliating their enemies in this way could be very important for the residents of a castle who were waiting out a long siege.

One of the primary roles of the ninja, and the one for which they are most well-known and feared, was that of assassin. The daimyo of feudal Japan came to fear assassination at the hands of ninja so much that they spent a great deal of time at "secret springs," which were hidden resorts built around natural springs far from the daimyo's castle.

Within the castle, a daimyo would often go to extraordinary lengths to protect himself from ninja. In Kyoto, the Nijo Castle sported "nightingale floors." These carefully crafted wooden floors were counterbalanced so that anyone walking on them made a loud squeaking noise. Some daimyo kept guards in the same room with them at all times, even when they were asleep. The Tokugawa family required everyone in the household to wear trousers with wide legs that dragged on the floor, making it impossible to walk quietly.

During the Tokugawa (or Edo) period (1603–1868), Japan's civil wars were halted by the strict controls of the Tokugawa shogun. Peacetime forced many people in Japanese society to find different roles, including the ninja. They were very useful to Tokugawa, acting as spies and bodyguards and helping to enforce the laws that allowed him to maintain control over the clans.

DEATH ON THE POT

Despite the daimyos' precautions to protect themselves from ninja tactics, ninja still brought death to many of them. One legendary story tells of a ninja who hid in the pit beneath his target's outhouse. When the daimyo arrived to use the bathroom, the ninja struck with his sword from below. However, this story is probably not true. Historical records show that the daimyo in question probably died from a stroke or a brain aneurysm.

➤ Supernatural Assassins?

Over the centuries, the ninja's fearsome reputation grew and grew. Eventually, the stories and legends surrounding them took on supernatural qualities. This happened in several ways:

➤ Historical figures and legendary heroes in Japan had ninja skills added to their stories.

➤ True stories of ninja exploits were expanded and exaggerated.

➤ The ninja themselves often used tricks and disguises that made their powers seem supernatural.

The ninja did little to discourage the myths that sprung up about them because these tales helped them to carry out missions and succeed in their secretive work. The mythical super-ninja supposedly were:

➤ Seven feet tall.
➤ Able to fly.
➤ Able to become invisible.
➤ Able to walk through walls.
➤ Shape-shifters.
➤ Three-headed.
➤ Ghosts.

➤ Ninja Gear

Ninja used a wide variety of weapons, as well as other specialized equipment, to help them survive alone on difficult missions.

A ninja's uniform is called a *ninja-yoroi*, or ninja armor. It consists of a black jacket, black trousers, light sandals, and a hooded cowl. Some ninja costumes included red accents along with the black, supposedly to hide any injuries the ninja might receive from his enemies. There is some evidence that ninja wore all white costumes in snowy conditions, but the multi-colored ninja seen in some action movies did not exist. A few ninja wore lightweight armor beneath their shirts.

Much of a ninja's work was not done while wearing his *ninja-yoroi*, however. Wearing a black hood would be too conspicuous for a ninja who needed to gather information or get close to an assassination victim in a crowded place. The ninja were experts at hiding in plain sight, disguising themselves as priests, dancers, merchants, or farmers. They tried to look as plain and ordinary as possible.

A ninja usually wore a *ninja-to* or other short sword on his back. They also used *shuko*, weapons worn on the hand (similar to brass knuckles), or tiger claws, sharp blades on the palm of the hand that may have been as effective for climbing as for hand-to-hand combat.

Ninja are famous for using *shuriken*, or ninja throwing stars. These were often small knives or daggers in addition to the well-known star shapes. The stars could not be aimed accurately and were usually just a delaying weapon if a ninja was being chased. Although the stars had little chance of striking their target, even the toughest pursuer might hesitate if he saw a sharp metal blade flying out of the darkness at his face.

The ninja also used an array of other weapons, including short knives, roped weapons for entangling a foe or striking from a distance, and weapons mounted on long bamboo poles. Some ninja may have used poison on their bladed weapons, though murky historical records make it difficult to tell if this is true.

Other useful ninja gear included rope ladders with hooks on the ends to throw up onto walls; small, sharp tacks called *caltrops* that could be left on the ground for enemies to step on (particularly useful in Japan, where most people wore no more than light straw sandals); small, one-person boats that could be folded down to a portable size; smoke bombs; blow guns; short hollow tubes for breathing under water; and special healing herbs in case the ninja was injured while on a mission.

➤ The Modern Ninja Craze

Japan rediscovered the ninja in the 1950s and 1960s. They became favorite characters in comic books and movies. The first appearance of a ninja in a popular Western work was in the 1964 James Bond novel, *You Only Live Twice*. When the movie version appeared in 1967, the popularity of ninja exploded across Europe and North America.

Since then, ninja have appeared everywhere. The G.I. Joe character Snake Eyes and his archenemy Storm Shadow were ninja. Martial arts star Chuck Norris fought off hordes of ninja in many of his popular action movies. The Teenage Mutant Ninja Turtles were pop icons in the late '80s and early '90s. And some martial arts schools have taken up ninja training as a separate discipline, alongside the more common forms of hand-to-hand combat training.

Modern equivalents of true ninja can be found in the special operatives and espionage agents used by military forces around the world. These elite troops combine combat skills, stealth, and technology to infiltrate enemy strongholds, gather secret information, and spread disinformation—just like their ninja forefathers did hundreds of years ago.

How Aborigines Work

Moving due south from Japan and its secretive ninja, we'll tackle the strange and amazing land of Australia and its first equally enigmatic inhabitants, the Aborigines. These "natives" were really the first people to set foot on the continent, somewhere between forty thousand and sixty thousand years ago. The Aborigines' creation story describes their arrival in terms of the Dreamtime, the beginning of time when the spirits created the world.

During Dreamtime, spirits rose from below the Earth and transformed into all the natural elements you see in Australia today—rivers, lakes, mountains, hills, and caves. According to Aboriginal beliefs, the spirits literally make up the land. The Aborigines see these spirits in much the same way as Christians view God or Muslims view Allah. However, the Aborigines believe that these spirits are alive within the land of Australia. Because of this, these indigenous people view the land as sacred and treat it as such.

The dreamings, or stories, of the Dreamtime are also considered sacred, and they're kept secret from the outside world. Elders draw these stories in a series, called a dreaming trail, using symbols. Young men then learn what the symbols mean and how to translate them so they can pass the history along to the next generation. Many Aborigines consider the dreamings to be the absolute truth—an unquestionable recording of history.

The scientific explanation for how Aborigines arrived in Australia is simple: they walked. Within the last decade, studies have proposed the possibility that all humans came from Africa within the past two hundred thousand years. A group of geneticists at the University of Cambridge in England built on that research by studying the DNA of Aborigines to determine when they arrived in Australia and from where.

According to Toomas Kisivild, PhD, and his team, the Aborigines walked from Africa into Eurasia. From there, they spread from India along the coastlines of Southeast Asia, where they then traveled over a land bridge connecting Australia to Asia. Once the seas rose and covered the land that connected the continents, the Aborigines were isolated for thousands of years.

What was life like for early Aborigines, and how did that change with the influx of English settlers? How do the struggle for civil rights in Australia compare to what's happened in other countries? Let's explore these questions and their implications for Aborigines and Australians today.

➤ Early Aboriginal Culture

Early Australian Aborigines were hunter-gatherers who prac-
ticed no farming techniques and kept no domestic animals.
They had limited weapons, mostly made of wood and stone,
to help them acquire their food. As in many other communities around the world, the men were the predominant hunt-
ers, killing large and small animals such as wallabies, emus, and
kangaroos. Women made an equal contribution by gathering
vegetables, fruits, roots, and small game like snakes.

In coastal areas, both men and women dove for shellfish.
They also used fibers and ropes to make baskets to catch
fish. Coastal Aborigines developed a type of boat that looked
like a flattened canoe. Because they were made of brush and
bark, these boats would become waterlogged after a period
of time. After only a few miles, they would begin to disin-
tegrate altogether.

As we discussed in the last section, the ancient Aborigines
worshipped their land and did everything they could to protect it. To preserve the land and its resources, most tribes
slept on the ground with no shelter. They hunted only what
they needed to eat and gathered only the plants and roots
they needed to sustain themselves. According to Aboriginal
beliefs, the spirits assigned the land itself to the various tribes.
Because of this, there were no territorial wars. If people were
on land that didn't belong to their tribe, they would begin

to feel the spirits' angry energy, and bad things would begin to happen.

For most of their existence, Aborigines also wore no clothes, which is amazing considering how cold parts of the continent can get in the winter. In the colder regions, men and women might keep themselves warm by draping themselves in animal pelts that were sewn together. In other areas, they might use what they could find, like animal fat or a clay called ocher, to protect their skin. Women often made necklaces using materials like shells. Their bodies were often canvases for artwork, with charcoal and ocher used as paint.

Music and dance were a large part of the culture, as was storytelling. Elders used all three to tell the stories of the dreamings, give thanks to the spirits, and even ask favors like increased fertility or rain. They also created musical instruments, the most famous being the didgeridoo. Creation of a didgeridoo begins when termites hollow out the inside of a piece of wood, which the Aborigines then cut to five feet. When played, the didgeridoo produces a low hum caused by vibrations. Various tribes use it in formal ceremonies and events.

The Aborigines kept this peaceful way of life for more than forty thousand years. But that all changed once the Europeans colonized Australia.

ABORIGINAL APPEARANCE

Due to their isolation, Aborigines haven't changed much in appearance since their arrival in Australia. Both ancient and modern Aborigines have dark skin and hair, which tends to be fairly straight or wavy. Their eyes are deep set, and the brow ridge hangs over the eye sockets. Their nose is typically broad and separated from the brow by a deep groove. A wide mouth and full lips spread up into dominant cheekbones. However, one change seems to have taken place: Aborigines of the past were tall, slender, and lean. The Aborigines of today tend to have a stockier, wider build.

➤ Colonizing the Land Down Under

Colonization was very similar to the colonization of the Americas. While some settlers traveled to the colonies voluntarily, the English government also used these outposts as prisons. Once the American Revolution began in 1776, England needed a new place to send its prisoners, since the American colonies would no longer take them. So in 1788, England sent a crew to Australia, then known as New South Wales, and began building prisons. This would mark the beginning of the fall of the Aborigines.

As with the Native Americans, the English quickly forced the Aborigines off their land. Many were beaten and killed. Others contracted diseases that were foreign to their immune systems and died. Starvation became a major problem. The Aborigines could no longer roam the land where they found their food, and many tribes died out completely. The English forced many of those who weren't killed into slavery. Women and children did everything from gathering food to cleaning for the settlers. Many women were also kept as sex slaves.

When the English arrived in 1788, the number of Aborigines was in the hundreds of thousands and possibly into the millions. With the deaths that followed the arrival of the English, the number of Aborigines dwindled drastically until only a few were left.

Unfortunately, over the next centuries things got worse before they got better. Besides losing hundreds of thousands of lives, the Aborigines lost much of their culture. They could no longer tell their stories and traditions, and in some cases, there was no one to hear them. History was lost. At the time of colonization, Aborigines spoke an estimated 250 to 300 different languages. More than half of these have disappeared altogether.

Then, in the early part of the twentieth century, non-indigenous Australians (anyone not an Aborigine) decided the only way to save the Aborigines was to assimilate them into the white Australian way of life.

THE WASTELAND: NEW SOUTH WALES

Australia was the last continent to be found by the Europeans. In 1768, James Cook left England to explore the South Seas. He came across Australia and proclaimed it New South Wales. He promptly left, and no one else ventured to the continent for two decades.

➤ We Have a Dream—and a Culture to Protect

The practice of slavery in Australia didn't end at the same time it did in the United States. There was no war, and there was no proclamation decreeing that all slaves must go free. In fact, slavery didn't end in Australia until the 1970s, and it took a different form than in the United States.

Beginning in 1910, non-indigenous Australians began to take Aboriginal children from their homes and families. These children, known as the Stolen Generation, were either given to white families—to be raised as white children—or to institutions and orphanages where they were forced to assimilate into white society. Between 1910 and 1970, when the practice stopped, more than one hundred thousand children were separated from their families and culture.

In 1967, following the example of the Civil Rights Movement in the United States, the Aborigines began to fight for equal rights. The white Australians—the only ones with the power to vote—passed a referendum to the Australian constitution that gave Aborigines the right to vote. The passing of the referendum also meant that Aborigines could be included in future censuses, officially recognizing them as citizens of Australia.

Aborigines are still fighting for equality in Australia, and racism is still prevalent throughout the continent. The life expectancy of the typical Aborigine lags almost twenty years behind that of the typical white Australian. Aborigines also still don't own most of the land that was taken from them during the colonial period.

STOLEN AWAY: BRUCE TREVORROW

In 1957, Bruce Trevorrow was taken from his family and given to a white family. He was thirteen months old. Meanwhile, his two brothers and two sisters remained with his parents. Trevorrow eventually sued the government for compensation and won. Trevorrow was the first member of the Stolen Generation to receive government compensation and was awarded $450,000 in 2007.

➤ Justice at Last

Over the past two decades, the Aborigines have tried to reclaim what was once theirs. Here are some of the major turning points:

- ➤ 1976—The Aboriginal Land Rights Act is passed, allowing the Aborigines to begin staking claims on land. This turned out to be a double-edged sword, however. To win rights to land, Aborigines had to prove that they were the first ones on it. To do this, they had to tell their history. But as we saw with the Dreamtime, Aborigines consider these stories sacred and secret. Aborigines had to make a choice between betraying their ancestors and taking back their land.

- ➤ 1995—The Human Rights and Equal Opportunity Commission launches the National Inquiry into the Separation of Aboriginal and Torres Strait Islander Children from Their Families, which results in recommendations for reparations and equal rights for Aborigines. At the time, the Australian government rejected all recommendations and refused to pay compensation.

- ➤ 1999—The Australian Parliament releases a statement stating that its members regret what happened to the Stolen Generation.

- ➤ 2006—An Australian court grants the Aborigines

land rights to almost 2,300 square miles of the major city of Perth.

➤ 2008—The Australian government announces its plan to formally apologize to the Stolen Generation of children in order to bridge the gap between Aborigines and non-indigenous Australians.

While all of these events have helped to usher in equality for the Aborigines, they have not left a perfect system in place. In the next section, we'll look at how the Australian Aborigines live today.

➤ The Modern Aborigine

As of 2011, the Aboriginal population had grown to more than 548,000, but that's still only 2.5 percent of the population of Australia. And although things are improving, there are still glaring inequalities between the races.

For the Aborigines who live in the major cities of Australia, alcoholism and violence are a way of life. Most Aborigines are very poor and have a very low standard of living. Aboriginal elders are attempting to change the violent tendencies of some of their young men by taking them to one of many sacred sites and teaching them the ancient ways of their people. The Australian educational system, which was once segregated, is now open to Aboriginal children, who are encouraged to attend. However, many Aboriginal children drop out at a young age.

The Aborigines who continue to live in the rural areas of Australia—or the outback—have tried to keep as much of their tradition and history alive as they can. Australians have attempted to build houses and other types of shelter for them. But for the most part, Aborigines use these structures only for storage.

Many of these traditional Aborigines are trying to spread their history to the members of their race who seem to have lost it. They've hired teachers to train students in the traditional Aboriginal languages. Even a few radio and TV stations feature only Aboriginal programming to educate the generations that have had no prior experience with their culture.

And of course, there's Aboriginal art. Their art is world famous, and many Aborigines make a living by selling their pieces. Traditionally, they viewed art much like their dreamings: sacred and secret. Only a select few people, after reaching a proper level of knowledge of Aboriginal history, were permitted to see the artwork. In recent years, though, that's changed so some artists can support themselves and their families.

Aboriginal art comes in many media: paintings, bead-work, woodwork, bark paintings, and baskets. Aborigines also make and sell the most famous item to come out of Australia: the boomerang. But some art can't be sold because it's on the walls of caves. A famous Australian landmark, Ayers Rock, is one such place. It's at an Aboriginal sacred site named Uluru, located near the center of Australia. The rock covers a series of caves. Within those caves are walls and walls of paintings done by the Aborigines to illustrate their dreamings. While people can visit Ayers Rock and see the paintings, there's no way to know what they mean. And the Aborigines, for the time being, are keeping that information a secret.

"No One Expects the Spanish Inquisition!": How the Spanish Inquisition Worked

As we saw in the previous section, history is plagued with persecution, violence, and destruction of culture. But one of the most famous examples of widespread intolerance, the Spanish Inquisition, may also have been the most surprising—at least according to Monty Python.

Have you ever heard someone say, "Nobody expects the Spanish Inquisition"? The line comes from a series of sketches by the British comedy troupe Monty Python. In the sketches, one character gets annoyed at another character for asking him question after question. At the height of his frustration, he yells, "Well, I wasn't expecting the Spanish Inquisition!" Suddenly, three Catholic cardinals burst into the room to comically "torture" the first two characters into admitting their sinful ways.

From the sketches, you can guess that the Spanish Inquisition must've involved torture and the Catholic Church. But why? Who was on the receiving end of that torture? And did anyone expect the Spanish Inquisition?

➤ Down With the Devil! The Beginnings of the Spanish Inquisition

The Spanish Inquisition began with religious intolerance and ended with torture—with false accusations and unfair trials in between. In truth, it was just one of several inquisitions that occurred between the twelfth and nineteenth centuries. Although early Christians experienced heavy persecution, by the Middle Ages, the Catholic Church had significant religious and political power in Europe. To maintain its authority, the Church suppressed heretics.

The Church had a very specific definition of heresy. A heretic publicly declared his beliefs (based upon what the Church considered inaccurate interpretations of the Bible) and refused to denounce them, even after being corrected by the authority. He also tried to teach his beliefs to other people. He had to be doing these things of his own free will, not under the influence of the devil.

DEFINE "INQUISITION"

Inquiring minds want to know: What does "inquisition" even refer to? In addition to the term being used for these historical events of prolonged persecution, the word "inquisition" refers to the tribunal court system used by both the Catholic Church and some Catholic monarchs to root out, suppress, and punish heretics—baptized members of the Church who held opinions contrary to the Catholic faith. The inquisitorial system was based on ancient Roman law. It was different from other court systems because the court actually took part in the process of trying the accused. The term "inquisition" also has a third meaning—the trials themselves.

The inquisitions officially began in 1231 when Pope Gregory XI issued a series of bulls, or decrees, that set up a tribunal court system to try heretics and punish them. Collectively, these decrees and the process became known as the papal inquisition. Pope Gregory chose the Dominican Order—known for being very well-educated and knowledgeable about complex theology—to conduct the inquisition.

The Spanish Inquisition three centuries later was unique in that it was established by secular rulers, King Ferdinand II and Queen Isabella, with the approval of Pope Sixtus IV. The monarchy was Catholic and had just united two kingdoms, Aragon and Castile, as a single country in the late fifteenth century.

Reasons for the Spanish Inquisition included a desire to create religious unity and weaken local political authorities and familial alliances. Money was another motive, since the government made a profit by confiscating the property of those found guilty of heresy. Historians speculate that the monarchy convinced Pope Sixtus IV to allow the inquisition by threatening to remove Spanish troops from Rome, where they were needed to prevent an attack by Turkey.

Many prominent Spanish citizens were concerned about their country's religious diversity and had bigoted attitudes toward non-Catholics. Jews were subjected to violent attacks known as pogroms and isolated in ghettos. Many were killed. The inquisition was officially established in 1478, and Jews were banished when King Ferdinand II issued the Alhambra Decree in 1492, ordering them to leave on pain of death. Many Jews converted to Catholicism. These converts were sometimes called *marranos* (a very derogatory Spanish term for "pig") and accused of secretly continuing to practice Judaism. They became easy targets of the inquisition.

Spain then conquered Granada, a region populated mostly by Muslim Moors. Muslims suffered opposition and persecution similar to that of the Jews, until they were banished in 1502 in the name of religious and cultural unity. Muslim converts to Catholicism, called *Moriscos* (Spanish for "Moorish"), were targeted for the same reasons as Jewish converts. In the late sixteenth century, Protestants, mainly Lutherans, also became a target of the inquisition.

The Spanish Inquisition spread to Spanish-controlled colonies in the New World, including Mexico. Centuries later, inquisition was finally abolished in Spain in 1834 by Queen Isabel II.

GALILEO AND OTHER INQUISITION TARGETS

Waldensians and Cathars, members of spiritual movements that gained popularity and threatened the authority of the Catholic Church, were the primary targets of the Medieval Inquisition.

The Portuguese Inquisition was similar to the Spanish Inquisition in that it operated under the monarchy. It was established in 1536 and targeted Jews and recent converts to Christianity, as well as accused witches. The Portuguese Inquisition extended to Portugal's New World colonies. A later Portuguese inquisition, the Goa Inquisition, targeted Hindus as well.

The Roman Inquisition, established during the 1540s, focused on the heretical crimes of witchcraft, sorcery, and blasphemy. One of its most famous cases was that of Galileo Galilei.

➤ Inquisition Trials and Tribulations

As mentioned earlier, the inquisitions were tribunals—a type of trial where the judge (or judges) tries the accused and passes judgment. But these trials were unique in several ways. The accused was required to testify, and he didn't get a lawyer or any assistance. If he refused to testify, the Inquisitor took this refusal as proof of his guilt. Anybody could testify against the accused, including relatives, criminals, and other heretics, and he wasn't told who his accusers were. The accused usually didn't have any witnesses testify on his behalf, because they could also fall under suspicion of being heretics. He also wasn't always immediately informed of the charges against him.

The inquisitorial court traveled the country conducting tribunals. This court consisted of two inquisitors as well as secretaries and other members. A typical inquisition began with an edict of grace after a Catholic mass, in which the inquisitors explained what constituted heresy and encouraged the congregation to confess any transgressions. Those that confessed escaped torture and extreme punishment but were forced to denounce any other heretics.

BAD COP, WORSE COP

A person who confessed and was convicted of a crime might be tortured again until he identified his accomplices. Critics of these criminal "justice" systems pointed out the absurdity of such a practice. If a person would confess to committing a crime themselves under torture, why would that person hesitate to accuse others while being subjected to incredible pain?

Heresy could be definitively proven if the accused was caught in a heretical act, but the goal of the inquisitor was always to extract a confession, or admission of guilt. Inquisitors were not only better educated and better versed in the Bible than their subjects; they were also specifically trained in how to question them in confusing or leading ways. Often, the accused wasn't clever enough to answer the inquisitor's questions and prove his innocence. But the inquisitor still needed a satisfactory confession. Accused heretics could be imprisoned for years until one was obtained.

In 1252, Pope Innocent IV had issued a bull that allowed the use of torture to get a confession. In the sixteenth century, the Spanish inquisitors quickly took advantage of this bull. This task was often assigned to local authorities, but the inquisitors themselves participated as well. If the accused confessed while being tortured, he had to confess again while not under torture in order for the confession to count. Torture was only supposed to be used if all other attempts at obtaining proof of heresy had been exhausted.

➤ Torture and Punishment During the Spanish Inquisition

Torture and punishment during the Spanish Inquisition were supposed to be rare, but they weren't. Technically, these methods were only to be used to get a confession, not to actually punish the accused heretic for his crimes. Some inquisitors used starvation, forced the accused to consume and hold vast quantities of water or other fluids, or heaped burning coals on parts of their bodies. But these methods didn't always work fast enough for the accusers' liking.

Strappado is a form of torture that began with the Medieval Inquisition. In one version, the hands of the accused were tied behind his back and the rope looped over a brace in the ceiling of the chamber or attached to a pulley. Then the subject was raised until he was hanging from his arms. This might cause the shoulders to pull out of their sockets. Sometimes, the torturers added a series of drops, jerking the subject up and down. Weights could be added to the ankles and feet to make the hanging even more painful.

The rack was another well-known torture method associated with the inquisitions. The subject had his hands and feet tied or chained to rollers at one or both ends of a wooden or metal frame. The torturer turned the rollers with a handle, which pulled the chains or ropes in increments and stretched the subject's joints, often until they dislocated. If the torturer continued turning the rollers, the accused's arms and legs could be torn off. Often, simply seeing someone being tortured on the rack was enough to make someone else confess.

While the accused heretics were on strappado or the rack, inquisitors frequently applied other torture devices to their bodies. These included heated metal pincers, thumbscrews, boots, or other devices designed to burn, pinch, or otherwise mutilate hands, feet, or bodily orifices. Although mutilation was technically forbidden, in 1256, Pope Alexander IV decreed that inquisitors could clear each other from any wrongdoing that they might have done during torture sessions.

TORTURE ON TRIAL?

Some courts used torture to determine if someone accused of a crime was truly guilty. This torture would take strange forms: someone's arm would be forced into boiling water, and the verdict would be based on how well the arm healed days later. Other courts simply tortured people to get them to confess to the crimes. The courts themselves even recognized, in their twisted way, that a confession given under torture held no legal meaning. Such a confession had to be confirmed by the victims while not being tortured within twenty-four hours. If they refused, they were simply tortured until they confessed again.

Inquisitors needed to extract a confession because they believed it was their duty to bring the accused back to the faith. A true confession resulted in the accused being forgiven, but he was usually still forced to absolve himself by performing penances, such as pilgrimages or wearing multiple, heavy crosses.

If the accused didn't confess, the inquisitors could sentence him to life imprisonment. Repeat offenders—people who confessed, then retracted their confessions and publicly returned to their heretical ways—could be "abandoned" to the "secular arm." Basically, it meant that although the inquisitors themselves didn't execute heretics, they could let other people do it.

Capital punishment did allow for burning at the stake. In some cases, accused heretics who had died before their final sentencing had their corpses or bones dug up, burned, and cast out. The last inquisitorial act in Spain occurred in 1834, but all of the inquisitions continued to have a lasting impact on Catholicism, Christianity, and the world as a whole. In the next section, we'll see how the Inquisitions are viewed today.

➤ The Tortuous Aftermath

While most people think of a single inquisition, history isn't quite that simple. Most of the inquisitions had little to do with creating unity. Instead, the goal was to maintain authority and discourage rebellious behavior.

The Protestant Reformation in the 1520s and other Christian reform movements contributed to the idea of a single inquisition masterminded directly by the Catholic Church. Because Spain was the greatest political power in Europe in the sixteenth century, reformers focused on the inquisitions that took place in that country. In some cases, they exaggerated circumstances of the inquisitions to increase anti-Catholic and, therefore, anti-Spanish sentiment.

In 1998, Pope John Paul II addressed the International Symposium on the Inquisition. In his address, he stated that "the Inquisition belongs to a tormented phase in the history of the Church, which…Christians examine in a spirit of sincerity and open-mindedness." However, the Pope also stated that "before asking for forgiveness, it is necessary to know the facts exactly and to recognize the deficiencies in regard to evangelical exigencies in the cases where it is so."

Six years later, the symposium released a report of its findings, which were based on studies of documents from the Vatican's Secret Archives. According to the symposium, most of the torture and executions attributed to the Catholic Church during the various inquisitions didn't occur at all. In addition, the total number of accused heretics put to death during the Spanish Inquisition comprised 0.1 percent of the more than forty thousand who were tried.

The number of witches burned at the stake by the inquisitions in Spain, Italy, and Portugal was ninety-nine, out of more than 125,000 trials. In fact, according to the symposium, in some cases the inquisitions saved lives by keeping accused heretics from secular authorities, who had both the power and desire to execute them.

Five Medieval Torture Devices

Torture was a very popular form of punishment in the Middle Ages, but it also served as a social deterrent and as entertainment for the masses. What really sets this time apart is the ghoulish inventiveness that gave rise to a plethora of torture methods. You've probably already heard about certain popular forms of torture—the rack, being burned at the stake, and finger-crushing thumbscrews—but these five devices show how creative torturers became with their tools.

➤ 1. The Brazen Bull

The Brazen Bull was a hollow brass statue crafted to resemble a real bull. Victims were placed inside, usually with their tongues cut out first. The door was shut, sealing them in. Fires would then be lit around the bull. As the victim succumbed to the searing heat inside, he would thrash about and scream in agony. The movements and sounds, muted by the bull's mass, made the apparatus appear alive, the sounds coming from inside like those of a real bull. This effect created additional amusement for the audience and distanced them from the brutality of the torture, since they couldn't directly see the victim.

Legend has it that this device was invented by a Greek named Perillus (Perilaus, according to some sources) for a tyrant named Phalaris of Agrigentum. Expecting a handsome reward for his creativity, Perillus instead became the first person placed inside the Brazen Bull. By some reports, Phalaris himself became an eventual victim of the bull when his subjects grew tired of his mistreatment.

➤ 2. The Scavenger's Daughter

A torture device commonly used to crack bones and dislocate the spine, the Scavenger's Daughter was invented by, and named after, a Brit named Skeffington. It is alternately referred to as Skevington's gyves. The apparatus consists of a hoop of iron with a hinge in the middle. The victim was forced to crouch on one half of the hoop while the other half was pivoted and placed over his back. (Imagine being placed into a giant set of iron dentures.) The torturer would use a screw to tighten the hinge, crushing the victim further and further into his involuntary crouch. Eventually, ribs and breastbone would crack and the spine could be dislocated. Sometimes the compression was so great that blood would gush from the fingertips and face. Queen Elizabeth I of England used this tool against Protestants she accused of high treason.

➤ 3. The Iron Maiden

The Iron Maiden is a device so fiendish that it was once thought to be fictional. It's an upright sarcophagus with spikes on the inner surfaces. Double doors open on the front, allowing entrance for the victim. In one example, eight spikes protruded from one door and thirteen from the other. Once the victim was inside, the doors were closed. There, the strategically placed spikes would pierce several vital organs. However, they were relatively short spikes, so the wounds wouldn't be instantly fatal. Instead, the victim would linger and bleed to death over several hours. To add to the abject horror of it all, two spikes were positioned specifically to penetrate the eyes.

In the 1800s, researchers found an Iron Maiden in a castle in Nuremberg, Germany, and documented proof of its use later surfaced. For this reason, this device is sometimes known as the Iron Maiden of Nuremberg. Other names included The Virgin and, in German, *Jungfrau*. A variation found in Spain was made to look like the Virgin Mary and had machinery that, when manipulated, caused her to "hug" the victim close to her spikes.

➤ 4. The Breast Ripper

Torturers seemed to reserve special horrors for women. Surprisingly, few torturers had any reservations about torturing women. In fact, women-only tortures often seemed especially cruel and were designed to destroy specific aspects of femininity. In medieval England, differing torture practices were virtually codified. Male criminals were hanged, while women faced the "drowning pits."

The practice of torturing women sexually extends back to Roman times (and surely even before then). Female victims were given to soldiers to be raped, or sent to brothels. They might be tied up or paraded through public streets naked. These public humiliations were sometimes followed by bizarre sexual mutilations. Torturers had a strange fixation on breasts, which were burned, branded, or simply amputated.

Worst of all was a device known as the Breast Ripper. It was a metal claw that pierced the flesh of the breast. The victim was tied to a wall, and then the claw pulled forcibly away, shredding the breast to pieces. It was used as both a method of punishment and interrogation—to mark the breasts of unmarried mothers and mutilate women convicted of heresy, adultery, and a host of other crimes.

➤ 5. The Pear of Anguish

It seems unlikely, but if anything could be worse than the Breast Ripper, it would surely be the Pear of Anguish. This was a pear-shaped device with the body of the pear made up of four metal "leaves" joined by a hinge at its top, and a key or crank on one end. The pear was inserted into the vagina, anus, or throat, depending on the nature of the crime committed. The oral device was reserved for heretics, while the anal and vaginal pears were used on homosexuals and witches, respectively. Turning the key opened the leaves, causing massive internal damage. The device was rarely fatal, but other methods of torture would usually follow.

In the next section, we move from secretive trials and tortures in Spain to a wide-open battlefield in France.

"All for One, One for All": How Musketeers Worked

My heart is that of a musketeer," declares d'Artagnan, the apprentice warrior from the sticks at the center of Alexandre Dumas's swashbuckling nineteenth-century novel, *The Three Musketeers*. Crammed with fighting, adventure, and lovemaking, the story follows d'Artagnan and the three "inseparables"—Athos, Porthos, and Aramis—as members of the Musketeers of the Guard under French King Louis XIII.

You may know this classic novel and the motto of its musketeers ("All for one, one for all") well. But did you know the story of musketeers—*real* musketeers—began in the 1600s, two centuries before they made their literary debut in 1844? What were these seventeenth-century soldiers fighting for?

The real Musketeers of the Guard were a group of soldiers who served as bodyguards to the king of France in the seventeenth century. The group takes its name from the musket, which was then an advanced form of military technology. In the 1600s, gunpowder weapons like the musket were expensive and sometimes elaborately decorated. They served as a prestigious emblem for the king's guard, making the group a formidable force, even though for everyday dueling, the musketeers were also skilled with a more traditional weapon: the sword.

➤ The Musketeers' Musket

During the late 1500s, the Spanish developed a firearm called the *moschetto,* or "sparrow-hawk." This was a long-barreled gun so heavy that it needed a forked stick to support the barrel. Other countries quickly adopted it—the French calling it a *mousquet*, the English a musket. It used a matchlock mechanism to fire a heavy bullet with enough force to crash through steel. Armored knights on horses, who had long ruled the battlefield, were suddenly sitting ducks for musketeers. They quickly faded from warfare.

A musketeer had to be strong to manage the unwieldy weapon, which could weigh up to 20 pounds (9 kilograms) and fire a ball almost an inch (2.5 centimeters) across. He also needed courage to master the complicated and dangerous process of loading and firing. With that combination, he was a warrior to be reckoned with.

Musketeers became deadly threats to knights. By the early 1700s, most soldiers were armed with these firearms, which continued to be called muskets, even though they had changed radically from the early days of the Spanish *moschetto*. The development of a lighter musket with a bayonet provided the weapon of most armies for more than a century. It's the firearm that was used in the American Revolutionary War. This new weapon also paved the way for the rise of the Musketeers of the Guard, the gallant troops who were the inspiration for the Dumas novel.

SWEET MUSKETEERS

The popularity of Dumas's novel made musketeers a household name. In 1932, the Mars candy company came out with a confection called "3 Musketeers." Originally, the candy consisted of three lumps of flavored nougat—strawberry, vanilla, and chocolate—each covered with milk chocolate. Later, the company eliminated the vanilla and strawberry and sold the candy as a single chocolate-flavored bar. But it kept the name.

➤ The French Musketeers of the Guard

Technically, all soldiers armed with muskets were musketeers. But the ones who wore the designation as a badge of honor were the personal household guards of French King Louis XIII. The king formed the Musketeers of the

Guard in 1622, a few years before the novel's plot begins. The musketeers of Louis XIII were soldiers who served as a combination of secret service and special forces. Their main duty was to protect the king and his family. In a time of frequent plots and conspiracies, this was no small task.

The early seventeenth century was a troubled period in France. French Protestants, known as Huguenots, opposed domination by the Catholic crown. Bitter religious wars broke out. The struggle for power among the king, the nobility, and the Church was constant, and assassination attempts were not uncommon. In fact, Louis's own father, Henri IV, had been assassinated in 1610.

Louis XIII became king of France when he was only nine. After assuming full power, he besieged the Huguenots in the port city of La Rochelle in the 1620s. The Musketeers of the Guard fought in that conflict, which is vividly depicted in Dumas's novel.

The musketeers were formidable warriors in battle. Their training and *esprit de corps* afforded them a decided edge. In later years, they wore elaborate uniforms trimmed with gold lace. The sight of their distinctive silver-embroidered blue tunics, not to mention their skill with powerful muskets, gave their enemies pause.

To become a Musketeer of the Guard, it helped to be an aristocrat or nobleman—not necessarily rich, but connected to the French ruling class. Over their long history, the number of musketeers in service varied from 150 to 300 men. The group served the French monarchy almost continuously until 1816, when it finally disbanded due to a lack of funding.

As a soldier, a Musketeer of the Guard was a specialist in the use of the musket. But did he always have one at hand? Definitely not. This large firearm had little role in protecting the king on a daily basis and was never used in the duels that the musketeers fought at the drop of a feathered hat. The sword was actually the common dueling weapon of a gentleman until it was replaced by the pistol in the late eighteenth century. The musketeers would have carried elegant rapiers at their sides. The Dumas novel is full of sword fights but only mentions musket firing a few times.

CARDINAL DIRECTION

Throughout his reign, King Louis XIII relied heavily on his chief minister, Cardinal Richelieu. This brilliant statesman largely directed French policy and held power second only to the king himself. The cardinal also formed his own guard of musketeers, who figure in the opening of *The Three Musketeers*. While Dumas depicts Richelieu as an enemy of the king in the book, in reality, the cardinal helped Louis XIII to consolidate royal power and guided France's diplomatic maneuvering through a war-torn era.

➤ Dumas's Dashing D'Artagnan and Co.

Alexandre Dumas was the grandson of a French nobleman and a Creole woman from Haiti. He began his career as a dramatist in Paris in the 1820s and went on to become one of the most popular novelists of his time.

Dumas adapted his famous story from an obscure, semifictional memoir about a musketeer named d'Artagnan. The real d'Artagnan joined the Musketeers of the Guard in 1632, later than his fictional counterpart, and served mostly under Louis XIV, who became king in 1643. D'Artagnan became commander of the Musketeers and was killed in war in 1673. The other main musketeer characters also had real-life counterparts, with names similar to those used in the novel. Dumas transformed the complicated history of the period into a story of love and adventure.

In the novel, d'Artagnan comes to Paris from rural Gascony bent on becoming a prestigious Musketeer of the Guard. He falls in with the Three Musketeers and becomes their close comrade. The musketeers are then drawn into a complicated intrigue involving Cardinal Richelieu, the English Earl of Buckingham, King Louis XIII, and Queen Anne. A secret agent known as Milady emerges as d'Artagnan's nemesis. The book abounds in tales of war, travels, romance, and adventure, with d'Artagnan becoming an official Musketeer along the way.

Like some modern authors of best-sellers, Dumas churned out books on an industrial scale. He wrote so voluminously that he had to employ assistants to help him. "But," as critic Terence Rafferty points out, "if Dumas was a hack, he was a hack with genius. His storytelling never seems the least bit mechanical: no assembly line, then or now, could ever turn out a narrative as joyful, as eccentric, as maddeningly human as *The Three Musketeers*."

The Three Musketeers has been adapted over and over into movies and stage productions. There have been comic versions, silent versions, and Technicolor extravaganzas. One of the latest big-screen renditions was a 2011 3-D film starring the actor Logan Lerman.

DUMAS HONORED

Whether because of his mixed-race ancestry or because he was more of a commercial writer than a literary one, Alexandre Dumas did not receive one of his country's highest honors until 2002. That year, by order of French President Jacques Chirac, Dumas's remains were moved to the Pantheon in Paris. Costumed musketeers carried his coffin. "Alexandre Dumas will finally take his place beside Victor Hugo and Emile Zola, his brothers in literature," Chirac said at the ceremony.

QUIZ: COULD YOU FIT IN AS A MUSKETEER?

T o be counted among the Musketeers of the Guard, a group of soldiers first selected hundreds of years ago to protect the king of France, a candidate had to be skilled in war, politics, and love. See if you could make the grade. Check your answers in the back of the book on page 226.

1. **The action in the novel *The Three Musketeers* takes place in what era?**
   a. The 1580s
   b. The 1620s
   c. The 1840s

2. **Who was Alexandre Dumas?**
   a. A minister of Louis XIII
   b. A popular novelist of the nineteenth century
   c. The founder of the Musketeers of the Guard

3. **At the beginning of the novel *The Three Musketeers*, who is d'Artagnan?**

   a. The leader of the Musketeers of the Guard

   b. A minister in the government of Louis XIII

   c. A poor boy from the sticks

4. **What was the motto of the three musketeers in the novel?**

   a. *Amor Vincit Omnia* (Love conquers all).

   b. All for one and one for all.

   c. Every man for himself.

5. **The original musket was a heavy firearm invented in which country?**

   a. Germany

   b. France

   c. Spain

6. **Which of the following was NOT a nougat flavor in the original 3 Musketeers candy bar?**

   a. Strawberry

   b. Mint

   c. Vanilla

7. **In duels, the musketeers relied mainly on which weapon?**

    a. The sword

    b. The pistol

    c. The musket

8. **What was a Huguenot?**

    a. A French sailor

    b. A French Protestant

    c. A French pastry

9. **True or False: The quintessential Musketeer's uniform included a blue tunic trimmed with gold lace and a three-cornered hat.**

    a. True

    b. False

10. **True or False: The Musketeers of the Guard still exist today as a ceremonial unit in France.**

    a. True

    b. False

How Witchcraft Works

While the musketeers were busy protecting their ruler in seventeenth-century France, British colonists across the Atlantic Ocean struggled to protect themselves from a far more nebulous and sinister threat: witchcraft. Witchcraft dates back countless centuries, and with all of the mythology floating around, it's hard to decipher fact from fiction. Were witches a real threat then—and do they still exist today? Do witches worship Satan? Do they cast spells? Are they good, like Glinda in the *Wizard of Oz*, or evil, like the Wicked Witch of the West?

In this section, we'll delve into the mysterious and hidden world of the modern witch, muddle through some of the witch's disputed history, find out why Halloween is a big night for them, and take a peek into some of their rituals.

The true definition of a witch, as well as the history of witches in general, is widely debated. Many texts describe witchcraft as pacts formed with the devil in exchange for powers to do evil and harm others. While this may be somewhat true of certain sects, most modern-day witches would describe it as far from their actual beliefs and practices.

Belief in magic and witchcraft has been around since the beginning of time. Early man paid tribute to the gods and goddesses that ruled his world and brought healthy crops and mild winters. The idea of magic came when things weren't so good. It grew from the chaos that accompanied bad weather, sickness, and shortages of food.

When times were bad, shamans, medicine people, witches, and other types of sorcerers would cast spells and perform rituals to harness the power of the gods. Harnessing this power had mixed results. Witches, who were primarily women, were originally seen as wise healers who could both nurture and destroy. However, this belief in their power eventually led to fear and often forced witches to live as outcasts, as we'll see in the next section.

OFFICIAL WITCHCRAFT

Roman law distinguished between good magic and bad magic. While bad magic (with the exception of murder) was punished with a fine, jail, or banishment, good magic (which was healing and divination) was officially sanctioned by Roman law.

➤ Witch Hunts

Once Christianity took hold in the late Middle Ages, the witches who performed magic were seen as devil worshippers who held Black Masses, hexed people, and flew around on brooms. This was also the time of the Reformation, which began as an attempt to reform the Roman Catholic Church but resulted in the creation of Protestant religions. Although the Reformation occurred primarily in the sixteenth century, it had its roots in the fourteenth century—about the time when the witch-hunt craze started.

Witch hunts in Europe and in the European colonies began around the 1450s and lasted until the 1750s. Because there were so many epidemics (like the Black Plague) and natural disasters, outbreaks of mass hysteria lead to pinpointing witches and witchcraft as the culprits.

During the various witch trials, prosecutors often used extreme torture to extract "confessions" from presumed witches. Innumerable witches were executed by public hanging or burning.

➤ The Salem Witch Trials

In 1692, in Salem, Massachusetts, an outbreak of witch hunts and witch trials started with strange behavior by two young girls. The girls were having convulsions and screaming that they were being pinched or bitten. The doctor who examined them eventually decided they were under some sort of spell or bewitchment. One by one, women in the town of Salem and even in surrounding areas began being accused of witchcraft.

The servant of one of the girls' families was West Indian and admitted in court to dealings with the devil, flying on "sticks," and being upset because "they" made her hurt those girls. This testimony clinched the hysteria that was already building. Salem residents were then certain that the devil was alive and very active in their land—and who knew what would happen next. Over nine months, more than a hundred people were imprisoned for being witches in Salem, and twenty were executed. Finally, a new court was constituted to replace the General Court, which had been holding the trials. This court, the Superior Court of Judicature, reversed the policy of the previous court. From this point on, only three more people were found guilty of witchcraft, and those three were later pardoned.

Theories today vary regarding what was actually wrong with the two young girls who started it all. Some say they were good actresses, and once they had started it and saw all of the attention they were getting, they had to keep it up. Another theory is that they actually had clinical hysteria, which would explain the convulsions. Or, as we'll see in the next section, there could be an entirely different explanation.

➤ Were the American Colonists Drugged During the Salem Witchcraft Trials?

The Puritans who conducted the witchcraft trials in Salem, Massachusetts, suspected that the devil was at work in their society. But could the madness have been caused by drugs?

One historian, Linnda Caporael, has suggested that perhaps a naturally occurring hallucinogen lay at the heart of one of the darkest moments in America's history. The hallucinogen is ergot, a toxic type of mold that is found in one of the staples of the human diet, grain. For centuries, farmers knew of the mold—which they called cockspur—but assumed it was harmless. However, simply eating bread containing flour made from grain containing ergot can kill a person.

Ergot poisoning can manifest in two ways:

1. Gangrenous ergotism, which involves a burning of the skin, blisters, and dry rot of the extremities, which eventually fall off. The condition usually results in the death of the sufferer.

2. Convulsive ergotism, which attacks the central nervous system, causing mania, psychosis, hallucinations, paralysis, and prickling sensations. These symptoms—especially the mania—reminded Caporael of those exhibited by Elizabeth Parris, one of the young girls at Salem.

Accounts written during 1692 describe behavior of the afflicted girls that bears an uncanny resemblance to a hallucinogenic state, and the fungus contains isoergine—the main ingredient in the drug LSD. Is it possible that Elizabeth Parris and her fellow afflicted had eaten tainted rye and fallen ill with convulsive ergotism?

Caporael researched the growing season of rye—the grain on which ergot seems to grow most easily—and found that there had been a wet summer in Salem prior to the winter of 1692. Ergot spreads most easily in damp weather. The historian also researched where the households of the girls got their grain. The first two afflicted, Elizabeth Parris and Abigail Williams, were cousins and lived beneath the same roof, so they both would have eaten the same grain. Moreover, two-thirds of the salary of their provider, the Reverend Parris, was paid in goods—like grain—rather than currency. The Parris household could have gotten the grain they ate from any number of sources.

The ergot-poisoning theory certainly seems to explain the afflictions the girls underwent, but the idea has come under attack since it was first introduced in 1976. Some historians feel that Elizabeth Parris, the first girl to fall ill, may indeed have suffered from some form of ergot poisoning. The rest of the girls, however, are believed to have taken an opportunity to stave off the boredom of colonial life with a ruse. If this is true, it's hard to imagine their reactions when the adults took the reins and began to hang their neighbors.

Other historians don't believe that ergot had anything to do with the Salem witch trials. University of Georgia history professor Peter Hoffer, PhD, raises some questions: "Why only the girls, why not others?" he asks. "Why only [1692], why not previous years and later years?" Hoffer, who has written extensively about the Salem witch trials, believes the girls who accused their neighbors of witchcraft were carrying out a prank.

Regardless of the cause—whether ergot poisoning, a teen prank, a vendetta against past wrongs, a grab for land, or mass hysteria—the Salem witch trials stand as a dark period in American history.

POINTY HATS

Where did the stereotypical hat style for witches come from? Some say it was simply the fashion around the time that witches began being characterized as evil, and therefore, more drawings were made of them wearing these hats. Others say the pointy hat represents a cone of power or a way of focusing power and energy. Modern witches may or may not don this accessory.

➤ Do Witches Still Exist Today?

Witchcraft is a pagan religion, meaning that its followers worship multiple deities rather than a single god. The word "pagan" actually stems from the Latin *pagini* or *paganus*, words meaning "hearth" or "home dweller" or, more simply, "country person." Those labeled as pagans were considered inferior to those living in cities. It didn't, however, mean those people were "bad." It wasn't until the 1450s that fear of witchcraft became more prevalent, and people began associating witchcraft and paganism with devil worship, evil hexes, and spells.

Many types of pagan witchcraft still exist today, some of which overlap and all of which can be defined in different ways by different people. Here are a few of the more popular, along with rough guidelines for their designations.

➤ **African witchcraft**—There are many types of witchcraft in Africa. The Azande of central Africa believe that witchcraft causes all types of misfortune. The "gift" of witchcraft, known as *mangu*, is passed from parent to child. Those possessing *mangu* aren't even aware of it and perform magick unconsciously while they sleep.

➤ **Appalachian folk magic**—Those who practice witchcraft in the Appalachian Mountains see good and evil as two distinct forces, one led by the Christian God and the other by the devil. They believe there are certain conditions that their magick cannot cure. They also believe that witches are blessed with paranormal powers and can perform powerful magick that can be used for either good or evil purposes. They look to nature for omens and portents of the future.

➤ **Green witchcraft**—A green witch is very similar to a *kitchen or cottage witch*, although the green witch practices in the fields and forest to be closer to the divine spirit. The green witch makes his or her own tools from accessible materials from outdoors.

➤ **Hedge witchcraft**—A hedge witch is not part of a group or coven. This witch practices magick alone and works more with the green arts, with herbal cures and spells. In the early days, hedge witches were local wise men or women who cured illnesses and gave advice. They can be of any religion and are considered *traditional witches*.

➤ **Hereditary witchcraft**—Hereditary witches believe in "gifts" of the craft that are with a witch from birth, having been passed from generations before.

➤ **Kitchen or cottage witchcraft**—A kitchen witch, or cottage witch, practices magick around the hearth and home. The home is a sacred place, and the herbs are often used to bring protection, prosperity, and healing. Kitchen witches often follow more than one path of witchcraft.

➤ **Pennsylvania Dutch hexcraft or "powwow"**—When the Germans first arrived in Pennsylvania, Native Americans were there, so using the term "powwow" to describe this practice may come from observations of Indian gatherings. Powwowing includes charms and incantations dating back to the Middle Ages, as well as elements borrowed from the Jewish Kabbalah and Christian Bible. Powwowing focuses on healing illnesses, protecting livestock, finding love, or casting or removing hexes. Powwowers consider themselves to be Christians endowed with supernatural powers.

➤ **Traditional witchcraft**—Traditional witchcraft often has science, history, and the arts as its foundation. While sharing the same respect for nature as the *Wiccan witch*, traditional witches do not worship nature nor the god or goddess of Wicca. They contact spirits that are part of an unseen spirit world during rituals. Magick is more practical than ceremonial and focuses greatly on herbs and potions. This sect of witchcraft does not have the law of harming none, but believes in responsibility and honor. Hexes and curses, therefore, can be used in self-defense or for other types of protection.

➤ **Wicca**—One of the modern pagan religions that worships the Earth and nature, Wicca is only about sixty years old. It was created in the 1940s and 1950s by Gerald Gardner. He defined witchcraft as a positive and life-affirming religion that includes divination, herb lore, magic, and psychic abilities. Wiccans take an oath to do no harm with their magick.

Most of those who call themselves witches today belong to the Wiccan religion, so we'll focus on Wicca for the duration of this section.

MAGIC VS. MAGICK

Books and other references about witchcraft use the spelling "magick" rather than "magic." While this spelling isn't in some dictionaries, it is the accepted spelling within Wicca (and possibly other pagan religions that use magic). The alternate spelling is to differentiate what the witch does from what a magician does—in other words, magic that invokes a deity to channel power as opposed to illusion. In this section, we will refer to the magic of witchcraft as "magick."

➤ Wiccan Witchcraft

Wicca, a modern pagan religion that worships the earth and nature, was established by Gerald Gardner as a positive and life-affirming religion. The central Wiccan theme is, "if it does no harm, do your own will." Gardner also ascribed to this definition many witchcraft practices and skills that had existed for centuries and been part of many different religions and cultures. These practices included such things as divination (foreknowledge), herb lore, magic, and psychic abilities. Modern witchcraft in Britain, Europe, North America, and Australia all evolved based on the Gardnerian definition and belief system. There are two major elements to Wicca:

- ➤ **No devil**—Wicca has no belief in a devil and does not subscribe to the Christian idea of hell, so the idea that modern witches worship the devil is nonsense.
- ➤ **Magickal energy**—The Wiccan belief is that when witches become one with the deities through rituals, they become in tune with the overall life force or cosmic energy. This allows the witch to somewhat control that energy (meaning the energy from themselves and their environment) and direct it for "personal" change through magick.

The magickal energy theory follows the scientific concept that all matter vibrates with its own energy. The speed of that vibration is dictated by the movement of the molecules that make up the object. Whether the object is solid or not is also determined by the movement of the molecules.

According to the book *Spellworking for Covens*, energy from the witch's body also has a vibration—both a physical rate of vibration and a spiritual rate of vibration. During power-raising rituals, witches believe that the molecules from both their physical and spiritual sides meld together to increase their overall energy and create a pathway for energy to flow through them. In order not to deplete their personal energy stores, they can also pull energy from the Earth and sky.

➤ Witches, Not Warlocks: Practicing Wicca

Practicing Wicca is about learning, not possessing a "gift." Both men and women can be witches. Men are also called witches, not warlocks. The word "warlock" actually means "oath breaker" and dates back to the witch hunts. It was used to refer to those who betrayed other witches, and in the witching world, the word still has a bad connotation.

A person does not need a natural or inherited "gift" or "talent" to be a Wiccan witch, only training. The Wiccan Rede is the witch's law and code of ethics. It says, in part, that witches should not perform magick that would harm another person. If they do, it will come back to them three-fold. So, if a witch hexes someone, he or she will experience misfortune that is three times worse. This is crucial part of the Wiccan belief, and one that is often seriously misunderstood. The magick they perform is supposed to be for personal change only.

TYPES OF MAGICK

Magick can be used for good or evil. The type of magick (black magick or white magick), along with the witch's intent, determines the outcome. Many witches, however, claim that black magick can be used for good, just as white magick can be used for bad—that it all depends on the intent.

Witches can either practice their craft in groups, called covens, or by themselves as solitaries. New members are welcomed into covens with a formal initiation ceremony. In the Gardnerian tradition, there are three phases of learning, each of which lasts a year and a day. Covens generally have their own rules, procedures, and names for these phases, but they tend to fall into the following categories:

1. Student, witch.

2. Practitioner, priest(ess).

3. Teacher, high priest(ess).

Once a new member has completed all phases, he or she is a full-fledged witch with the power to perform and participate in formal rituals.

In the next section, we will explain the basics of the Wiccan rituals. But before we get into that, let's take a look at some of the different tools of the witch's trade.

➤ Witch Accessories

Here are some of the accessories traditional witches or Wiccan followers might use:

Athame (Knife)

A knife isn't one of the traditional witch's props you can get at the costume shop, but the athame is an important part of many rituals. It is a double-edged knife with a blade about six inches long and not terribly sharp. The athame is used to mark the edges of the circle used in rituals and to stir the salt and water that are used to consecrate (or make sacred) the circle. It is also used sometimes to carve symbols or words into candles. The athame's owner marks either the handle or the blade with his or her witchcraft name and stores it in a white container or cloth. The athame is also used in the Great Rite ritual (more on the Great Rite later) as a phallic symbol, representing one half of the union of the God and Goddess from which new life comes.

Besom (Broom)

Witches don't actually fly on brooms, although many have them. They're used to purify an area of lingering energies (similar to the use of *sage*) before "casting a circle." Circles are cast before any ritual.

Book of Shadows

The Book of Shadows is essentially the witch's guidebook. It contains all of a particular witch's (or coven's) ritual and spell information. It is the written record of everything the witches in that coven need to know, such as descriptions and explanations of all of the sabbats. (More on sabbats later.)

Candles

When a circle is cast for a ritual, there are four quadrants representing north, south, east, and west. Quarter candles of specific colors are used: north is green (earth); south is red (fire); east is yellow (air); and west is blue (water). The candles are placed at the perimeter of the circle. Three candles are also used on the altar. The color of these candles represents the ritual being performed.

Cauldron

The cauldron is a necessary part of witches' paraphernalia. While many years ago, cauldrons were a part of every home, now they're seldom seen except at Halloween or as a yard decoration. But cauldrons with magical powers go back to the myth of the Celtic goddess Cerridwen, whose cauldron represented the cycle of birth, renewal, rebirth, and transformation. Witches today often burn small fires (balefires) or incense in their cauldrons. The cauldron can also represent the womb during the Great Rite ritual, which calls up the union of the God and Goddess from which new life comes.

Chalice

A chalice (cup) is used in ceremonies to represent the female principle of water. The chalice can also be used in place of the cauldron in performing the Great Rite, as well as in a "Cake and Ale" rite where a cup of wine is blessed by the High Priest and passed from member to member in the circle.

Clothing

Clothing is optional for most rituals, although most covens

require that everyone be in agreement about going skyclad (naked) before anyone does. Otherwise, witches wear long, hooded robes of varying, usually dark, colors.

Paton

An altar paton is a plate (or disk) of either metal or wood with a pentagram design on it. It is used on the altar to hold the tools needed for the ceremony and to act as a focal point.

Pentacle/Pentagram

The pentacle is a five-pointed star (a pentagram) enclosed within a circle. The "upright" pentacle or pentagram (one point up, two points down) is a widely recognized symbol of witchcraft. The points represent earth, fire, water, air, and spirit. The circle represents the God and Goddess that allow the energy of the pentagram to be focused. It is symbolic of the idea of bringing together spirit and earth.

Sage

Before a ritual, the area must be purified. Sage is often used (as is a *besom*) to cleanse the area of unwanted energies. When burned, the sage creates a thick, grayish smoke.

Salt Container

Another purifying agent is salt. The salt is usually in either a seashell or a glass dish. Salt is mixed with water to represent the elements of earth and water in order to consecrate the circle.

Staff

Witches can use a staff like they would a wand. The staff is usually shoulder height.

Sword

Some witches choose to use a sword rather than an athame to mark the boundaries of the circle.

Thurible (Incense Burner)

Incense represents the element of air. When burned, it also represents fire, both of which are used to purify the area or the tools being used. The thurible is often a small cauldron of metal or any other fire-resistant material.

Wand

Many witches use wands. Wands represent fire and the life force of the witch. A wand is a symbol of power, wisdom, and healing. Like the sword, staff, and athame, the wand can be used to cast the circle. It may also be used to direct energy during a spell.

Water Container

The water container used in the consecration of the circle can be any type of container as long as it is large enough to hold three pinches of salt and be stirred with the athame. Water is another purification agent.

➤ As If by Magic: Wiccan Ritual Preparation

Wiccan ritual preparation involves a series of steps, from purifying to calling the quarters to invoking the deity. Here, we'll explore a ritual preparation, which is a basic outline of the Gardnerian tradition of Wicca. Other traditions borrow extensively from this method, but they do have variances.

Note: What follows is a representation of the steps that may be followed in carrying out a ritual. Like any religion, different sects have different methods, and there is no single "right way" of holding a ceremony.

Necessary tools for the modern ritual to celebrate Mabon, the autumnal equinox, include a pentacle and incense. Here are the steps in the ritual preparation.

- ➤ **Purifying**—The first thing witches do is purify a circular area to get rid of any unwanted energy or forces. A witch may use a broom (besom) to sweep the area or burn a bundle of sage, holding it over his or her head while walking in a spiral pattern around the circle and then pausing at each of the four quadrants (north, south, east, and west). Each witch participating in the ritual is also purified by waving incense around his or her body.

➤ **Setting up the altar**—The altar is set up at the east side of the circle with candles to represent the God and Goddess, salt and water for purification, the athames of the High Priest and Priestess, and incense. Quarter candles are placed at each of the four quarters of the circle.

➤ **Casting the Sacred Circle**—The High Priest and Priestess cast the Sacred Circle. The Sacred Circle is considered to be a spot that is without place or time. The circle is cast by marking its edges with an athame or another tool such as a staff, sword, or wand. The area is purified again with salt and water. Three pinches of salt are placed into the water, which is stirred nine times with the athame. Then, this salty mixture is sprinkled around the perimeter of the circle. Incense is then lit and carried around the perimeter of the circle.

➤ **Calling the quarters**—The witches call together the spirits of the four elements: earth, fire, water, and air. The elements are the guardians that guide and protect the witches.

➤ **Invoking the deity**—A deity has to be involved to perform magick, so at this point in the ritual, the deities are called. Depending on the ritual, it could be either

the God, the Goddess, or both. They are called by recit-
ing invocations related to the specific ritual.

Everything up to this point has been preparation for the
ritual. At this time, the witches begin the actual ritual they
are performing. The Great Rite is a central one that we'll
explore here.

The Great Rite ritual represents the sexual union of
the God and Goddess, from which new life comes. This
union is not only to bring good harvest, but is also to continue the circle of life so that the new God can be born at
Yule. (See the next section to learn about Yule.) When
this rite is performed, it can be symbolic—using the athame
and cauldron to represent the sexual union—or the sexual
act can be performed by the High Priest and Priestess. If
the sexual act is to be performed, the entire coven must
agree that they want the Great Rite carried out in that way.
The actual union is performed in private, *not* with the rest
of the coven present, as is often assumed. Often, the High
Priest and Priestess are married.

More common is the symbolic version of the Great Rite.
In this version, the cauldron or chalice represents the womb
and is held by the High Priestess. The athame is the phallic
representation and is held by the High Priest. This rite may
vary, but in some covens it follows that the High Priestess

kneels at the altar with the cauldron in her hands facing the High Priest. The High Priest faces her with his athame.

Each recites lines to bring the Sun King to dance with the Maiden of Spring. Then, the High Priest lowers the athame into the cauldron as they both recite words of the Land of Youth, the Wine of Life, and the Cauldron of Cerridwen. The High Priest then takes the cauldron, holds it up in the air, and proclaims that this rite symbolizes the union of the God and Goddess.

Once the ritual is complete, the circle must be closed. The steps of casting the circle are reworked, only backward. The invoked deities are thanked for their help; the quarters are released; and the High Priest or Priestess "takes down" the circle by walking around the perimeter (in an opposite direction from before) with his or her athame pointed outward.

➤ Wiccan Holidays: It's More Than Halloween

Wiccan holidays are called sabbats, and they celebrate the eternal cycle of life. The Wheel of the Year is essentially the Wiccan calendar, and it shows the never-ending cycle.

The Wiccan year begins on the sabbat (holy day) of Yule, when the Goddess gives birth to the God. The God grows strong through spring and summer, and then in fall, the God and Goddess unite. At this time, the Goddess becomes pregnant with the new God. The old God dies on Samhain (Halloween) to be reborn at Yule. This cycle is acted out symbolically during certain rituals and is known as the Great Rite (see previous section).

There are eight sabbat rituals throughout the year:

➤ **Yule**—Celebrated at the winter solstice, Yule is the celebration of the Goddess giving birth to the God.

➤ **Imbolc**—Celebrated on February 2, it is the time when the first plantings of spring crops occur. It is also considered to be a time of spiritual cleansing and renewal of vows.

➤ **Ostara**—Celebrated at the spring equinox in March, this sabbat represents a new beginning, partly because it marks the beginning of longer days and shorter nights. It also marks the union of the God and Goddess and therefore symbolizes fertility.

➤ **Beltane**—Celebrated on May 1, it represents the end of the planting season and the beginning of harvesting. It also represents fertility, as the celebration often involves loosened rules for fidelity.

➤ **Litha**—Celebrated at the summer solstice, this sabbat represents the peak of the God's strength. It may involve lighting large bonfires to ward off evil spirits.

➤ **Lughnasadh**—Celebrated on August 1, this is a time when the Goddess turns over control to the God. It is a time of feasts and craft festivals.

➤ **Mabon**—Celebrated at the autumn equinox, Mabon represents the balance between light and dark, as it is the day that nights start becoming longer than days. It is officially the pagan day of Thanksgiving.

➤ **Samhain**—Celebrated on Halloween, Samhain means the end of summer and the beginning of winter. On this night, the dead are said to be able to communicate with the living in order to be with and celebrate with their families.

So now you've had a small peek into the world of modern Wiccan witches. Perhaps they're not as scary as they once seemed? But witchcraft isn't the only historical event with a tortured past, as we'll see in the next section.

QUIZ: THE ULTIMATE WITCHES QUIZ

G rab your broomsticks and black cats because it's time for the Ultimate Witches Quiz! Find out the hocus pocus behind the Salem witch trials, witches today, and other magical facts. Check your answers in the back of the book on page 228.

1. The word "pagan" comes from the Latin *pagini*, which means what?
   a. Evil
   b. Home dweller
   c. Flying object

2. During the Salem witch trials in 1692, the two girls who accused women of practicing witchcraft may have suffered from what condition?
   a. Epilepsy
   b. Tourette's syndrome
   c. Clinical hysteria

3. **How long did witch hunts last in Europe?**

   a. 50 years

   b. 150 years

   c. 300 years

4. **What is a witch's broomstick used for?**

   a. To fly

   b. To purify something

   c. To cast a spell

5. **The Wiccan religion, which draws on ancient pagan beliefs and rituals, was created when?**

   a. 1660s

   b. 1820s

   c. 1940s

6. **True or False: A "warlock" is a male witch.**

   a. True

   b. False

7. **The magic of modern witchcraft is technically referred to as what?**
   a. Magick
   b. Sorcery
   c. Hexing

8. **If Wiccans perform magick intended to harm someone else, what will supposedly happen?**
   a. The devil will visit them.
   b. They'll be banned from the coven.
   c. Their evil magick will return to them threefold.

How Prohibition Worked

Beer. Wine. Liquor. Hooch. Moonshine. Whatever kind of alcohol you prefer (or don't, for that matter), you can't argue that it has a pretty strong grip on American society. The alcohol industry spends more than $2 billion a year on advertising—bombarding TV watchers with racy commercials, splashing beer logos around stadiums, and sponsoring NASCAR race cars. It's hard to believe that less than a century ago, a country that now so clearly embraces alcohol tried its best to completely abolish it.

From 1920 to 1933, the Eighteenth Amendment to the United States Constitution forbade the sale, manufacture, and importation of alcohol. (Interestingly, the actual act of drinking it was not illegal.) This thirteen-year period was called Prohibition. Support for the legislation had been gaining ground for decades through the anti-alcohol efforts of the temperance movement, which finally achieved its goal of a nationwide ban.

The United States was a very different place when Prohibition was enacted. World War I was just coming to a close, and women and minorities still lacked the right to vote. So why did so many people spend so much time and effort trying to get rid of alcohol? In this section, we'll look at why and how Prohibition was enacted. We'll also discover how it affected the economy, organized crime, and corruption—and how it was eventually reversed, much to the relief of future fraternity boys everywhere.

TIMELINE: THE EARLY ROOTS OF PROHIBITION

➤ **1838**

Massachusetts creates a law making it only possible to buy hard liquor in large quantities, effectively preventing working-class citizens from purchasing it.

➤ **1846**

Maine becomes the first state to pass a statewide prohibition law. This encourages other cities and counties to go "dry."

➤ **1850s**

The First Reform Era begins with the intention of bringing change to certain areas of society, namely abolishing slavery. The anti-alcohol movement follows suit, with Irish and German immigrants the focus of reformers. Many of the initial successes happened in rural America, specifically in the Western and Southern states. Big-city folk were not nearly as interested in giving up alcohol as those in the Bible Belt were.

➤ 1861–1865

The Civil War sucks some of the life out of the prohibition cause, albeit temporarily. After the war ends, a boom in the liquor industry leads to increased alcohol consumption and rekindles the prohibition movement's fire.

➤ 1869

The Prohibition Party is formed when political advocates grow tired of Republicans and Democrats avoiding the issue. The party platform contended that outlawing alcohol would be the end of social and political corruption.

➤ 1873

The Women's Christian Temperance Union is formed when seventy women from Hillsboro, Ohio, pray on the floor of local saloons after a rousing pro-temperance sermon at a church. Eventually, the group's membership spread nationally, and it became a major political force.

➤ The Temperance Movement

The idea of banning alcohol in the United States started to pick up steam in the 1830s, long before Prohibition. Many people believed that alcohol was strongly connected to insanity, poverty, and many of the world's evils, so the temperance movement gained momentum. The number of people opposed to "demon rum" grew exponentially. Before long, thousands of societies sprouted up that were dedicated to promoting temperance. Hundreds of thousands of supporters helped spread the word, and early temperance laws began to take shape.

HELPFUL PROHIBITION-RELATED TERMS

> **Temperance**—Enjoying healthful things in moderation and abstaining completely from unhealthful things.
> **Moonshine**—Illegal alcohol distilled at home.
> **Wets**—Those opposed to prohibition.
> **Drys**—Those in favor of prohibition.
> **Bootlegging**—The illegal manufacture, sale, and transportation of alcoholic beverages.
> **Speakeasies**—Illegal drinking establishments.
> **Bathtub gin or hooch**—Moonshine.
> **Rum runners**—People who smuggled alcohol.

> **Giggle water**—Alcohol.
> **Setup**—Soda or ginger ale served in speakeasies. Patrons then added alcohol from a hip or thigh flask.

The groups dedicated to encouraging temperance had a number of reasons for it. They believed there was a direct link between alcohol and many antisocial behaviors, like child abuse and domestic violence. Another famous concern was that of Henry Ford, who believed that alcohol had a negative impact on labor productivity.

Anti-German sentiment during World War I helped to catapult the issue into law. Many of the nation's breweries were operated by German immigrants, known as "alien enemies" by the Anti-Saloon League. The sentiment was that the grain being produced should be used to feed soldiers rather than to produce alcohol.

But many others fought this growing issue tooth and nail. The Association Against the Prohibition Amendment and the Women's Organization for National Prohibition Reform were just two of these groups. Despite the efforts of anti-prohibition groups, support gathered for a ban on alcohol, and Congress eventually passed the Eighteenth Amendment on January 16, 1919. (The amendment went

into effect in 1920.) The amendment prohibited the manufacture, sale, export, import, and transportation of alcoholic
beverages but stopped short of banning personal possession
and consumption. Basically, if your wine cellar was already
stocked, you didn't have much to worry about.

In truth, the Eighteenth Amendment simply brought
to a national level what was already accepted in many
states. Sixty-five percent of the country, including nineteen states, had already banned alcohol on a local level.
The Volstead Act, or National Prohibition Act, was crucial
to the amendment's success because it provided the federal
government with enforcing ability. It also defined criminal
penalties, exceptions (medicinal and religious-ceremony
use), and the alcohol levels that qualified as "intoxicating."
Any beverage with more than 0.5 percent alcohol was over
the legal limit.

THE ORGANIZED CRIME CONNECTION

Once alcohol was made illegal, people had to find
other ways to get it. Enter organized crime, specifically
Al Capone. Chicago-area gangster John Torrio took
Capone under his wing, and Capone eventually took
over Torrio's organization, bringing the crime ring of
brothels, speakeasies, breweries, and distilleries to new

heights. At the peak of his success, his "businesses" yielded more than $100 million a year. Eventually, the corrupt mayor, who had decided not to fraternize with Capone anymore, forced him out of Chicago. Despite a morbidly impressive résumé of murder, smuggling, bribery, and other crimes, Capone served only a short time behind bars for tax evasion. He was eventually released for health reasons and died in 1947 of cardiac arrest following complications from syphilis.

➤ Look the Other Way: The Realities of Enforcing Prohibition

In a perfect world, once a law or constitutional amendment is passed, the resources necessary to enforce it are plentiful and effective. Unfortunately for its supporters, Prohibition was not so easily enforced. Many challenges quickly surfaced when the time came to keep demon rum from being bought, sold, or imported.

➤ Gangs of illegal alcohol traffickers, comparable to today's illegal drug rings, became common. They were able to charge a steep price for sneaking alcohol into the country—and they thrived in the process.

➤ The demand for $10,000 notes reached an unprec-
edented level in 1926. Critics of Prohibition identified this as a telltale sign of large transactions between
bootleggers.

➤ European "rum fleets" proliferated. Small boats would
sail out to ships waiting in international waters and bring
large quantities of alcohol back into the United States.
Smuggling alcohol from Canada was also very easy.

➤ Political corruption reached new levels, as those who
were profiting from illegal trafficking lined the pockets
of crooked politicians.

➤ Illegal speakeasies flourished. Prior to Prohibition, there
were fewer than fifteen thousand legal bars in the United
States. By 1927, however, more than thirty thousand
speakeasies were serving illegally across the country.
Approximately one hundred thousand people brewed
alcohol illegally themselves.

➤ Undercover police officers were trying to do their jobs,
but the available manpower was still tiny in comparison
to the thriving industry. Even when arrests were made,
corruption made it nearly impossible to convict anyone.
For example, during one period, more than seven thousand arrests were made in New York for alcohol viola-
tions, but only seventeen of those ended in conviction.
Many states eventually grew tired of the hassle. In fact,

by 1925 six states had developed laws that kept police from investigating infractions. Cities in the Midwest and Northeast were particularly uninterested in enforcing Prohibition.

Fiorello LaGuardia, mayor of New York City, had this to say in testifying before the Senate judiciary committee: "It is impossible to tell whether Prohibition is a good thing or a bad thing. It has never been enforced in this country."

➤ The Black Market of Booze

As we mentioned, Prohibition created a vast illegal market for the production, trafficking, and sale of alcohol. In turn, the economy took a major hit, thanks to lost tax revenue and legal jobs.

Prohibition nearly ruined the country's brewing industry. Anheuser-Busch survived Prohibition by turning to other products, such as ice cream, root beer, malt extract, and corn syrup. The city of St. Louis boasted twenty-two breweries before Prohibition, but a mere nine reopened after it ended. In desperation, people also took to manufacturing their own alcohol, often with deleterious effects.

The advent of the Great Depression (1929–1939) caused a huge change in American opinion about Prohibition. Economic issues crippled the country, and it just didn't make sense to those suffering that the country couldn't profit from the legal taxation of alcohol. After all, the gangsters and bootleggers certainly seemed to benefit.

Prohibition also produced some interesting statistics concerning the health of Americans.

➤ Deaths caused by cirrhosis of the liver in men dropped to 10.7 men per 100,000 from 29.5 men per 100,000 from 1911 to 1929.

➤ On the other hand, adulterated or contaminated liquor contributed to more than fifty thousand deaths and many cases of blindness and paralysis. It's fairly safe to say this wouldn't have happened in a country where liquor production was monitored and regulated.

➤ Alcohol consumption during Prohibition declined between 30 and 50 percent.

➤ Conversely, by the end of the 1920s there were more alcoholics and illegal drinking establishments than before Prohibition.

PROHIBITION IN HOLLYWOOD

Al Capone died over sixty years ago, but the gangster legend lives on in scores of movies, books, and TV shows. *Little Caesar* was an immensely popular film about 1920s gangsters that helped spawn a heap of others. Following the movie's release in 1930, more than fifty other gangster movies were released in the next year alone. True and fictional stories from that time have yielded many other incredibly popular films, like *The Godfather*, *Scarface*, and *Public Enemy*. And country bootleggers are often depicted as folk heroes—think *The Dukes of Hazzard*.

Roaring '20s style, immortalized in F. Scott Fitzgerald's *The Great Gatsby*, also has its place in TV and movie history. Hard-partying flappers—and their short hair, fringed dresses, and hip flasks—are still glamorized today, most recently in the movie musical *Chicago* and the 2013 movie remake of *Gatsby*. Flappers even had their own lingo, which rivals our slang today.

➤ Not a Dry Place in Town: Prohibition Ends

It takes one constitutional amendment to undo another. Enter the Twenty-First Amendment, the first—and, so far, only—amendment to restore rights taken away by a previous amendment. In 1932, both political parties called for the

Eighteenth Amendment to be repealed. In 1933, Congress answered by passing a resolution proposing the repeal. Once three-fourths of the states had ratified the resolution, the Twenty-First Amendment was passed, and alcohol began to flow again legally in the United States.

By December 5, 1933, when the amendment was ratified, even people who had vocally supported Prohibition had changed their tune dramatically. Their opinions about the evils of alcohol remained, but they had realized that the effects of Prohibition were far-reaching and perhaps worse than alcohol itself. According to famous tycoon John D. Rockefeller, "Drinking has generally increased, the speakeasy has replaced the saloon; a vast army of lawbreakers has been recruited and financed on a colossal scale."

After Prohibition was repealed, the states were left to decide how to govern alcohol consumption. Most states made twenty-one the legal drinking age, although a handful required drinkers to be only eighteen. No national drinking age existed until 1984, when the National Minimum Drinking Age Act was passed, setting the minimum age at twenty-one. One major catalyst behind the creation of this law was the increase in deaths related to drunk driving.

The 1980s and 1990s saw a major movement to decrease drunk driving. In 1980, Candy Lightner founded Mothers

Against Drunk Driving (MADD) after a drunk driver fatally hit her daughter. Since then, alcohol-related driving fatalities have decreased substantially. In 1982, 60 percent of automobile-related fatalities involved alcohol. By 2005, that number had dropped to 39 percent.

Despite the national repeal of Prohibition, hundreds of counties in the United States still enforce "dry" laws. These laws typically ban the manufacture and sale but not consumption.

- ➤ Nearly half of Mississippi's counties are dry. In fact, it's against the law to drive through a dry county in the state with alcohol in the car, even if you're transporting it to a personal residence.
- ➤ Kentucky isn't much better for alcohol lovers. Thirty counties are wet and fifty-five are bone-dry. The other thirty-five are considered "moist"—they have some regulations but not complete prohibition.
- ➤ Alabama, Arkansas, Texas, Kansas, and Virginia also have a large proportion of dry counties.
- ➤ Hundreds of dry towns (within wet counties) also exist across the country. In fact, 129 of them are in Alaska.

Many, many other rules exist regulating the sale and consumption of alcohol on a local level. They often seem confusing and contradictory. One other once-common rule restricts the sale of alcohol on Sundays. This law was developed in Colonial times to honor the Christian Sabbath day.

FAMOUS FIGURES OF PROHIBITION

> **Dr. Benjamin Rush**—Well-respected physician who was one of the first people to document the ill effects of gin, whiskey, and other distilled liquors. He was a staunch advocate of "personal cleanliness."

> **Carrie Nation**—As a leader of the Women's Christian Temperance Union, she was known for praying on the doorsteps of saloons and often brandishing a hatchet to scare off would-be drinkers. Her passion was fueled by a short-lived marriage to an alcoholic. She was arrested at least thirty times between 1900 and 1910 for destroying saloons with her pro-temperance cohorts.

> **Fatty Arbuckle**—In 1921, this famous screen actor was accused of raping an intoxicated aspiring actress who later died of peritonitis from a ruptured bladder. The theory was that he had raped her with a piece of glass or a bottle. Several trials later, Arbuckle was acquitted, but his career

was largely ruined. More than a decade later, he broke back into the industry but soon died of a heart attack.

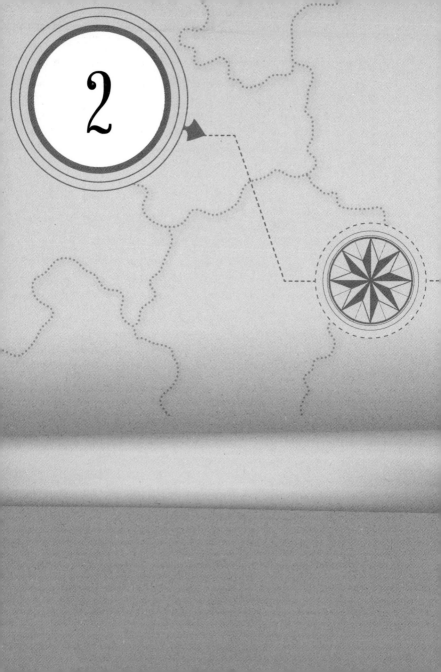

Scandals, Lies, Thefts, and Crimes

Now that we've demystified some of the strangest and most unique chapters in the history of mankind, it's time to delve into the juicier side of humanity. The biography of the human race is littered with stories of corruption, greed, vice, crime, and a healthy dose of stupidity. In this section, we'll take a look at some of the greatest—and dumbest—scandals, lies, thefts, and crimes, over the past five hundred years.

Top Five Marie Antoinette Scandals

Her subjects called her Madame Déficit, and they snickered at the dismal state of affairs in her royal bedroom. Marie Antoinette's death may well be the most well-known scandal of her life, but what are the other juicy details?

When Marie Antoinette died under the heavy blow of the guillotine on October 16, 1793, it was a decidedly unglamorous affair. That's not to say it wasn't a celebration: many French revolutionaries were ecstatic to bid the extravagant queen adieu forever. After the blade came down, the executioner brandished Marie Antoinette's head in a triumphant wave so that the entire crowd could see it.

Yet for the thousands of people gathered to watch the scene, it was a disappointment. They'd wanted to see the thirty-eight-year-old woman quake in fear and cower penitently. A well-known eighteenth-century journalist and revolutionary, Jacques Hébert, wrote in the newspaper *Le Père Duchesne* that she was "bold and impudent to the very end." Despite the fact that the executioner had cut off all her hair and ordered her to don a threadbare white shift (likely soiled by the time she made it up the steps to the guillotine—she'd been hemorrhaging for days), she maintained her composure.

Marie Antoinette's death was one of the biggest scandals of her life. Was it good riddance or not? To this day, there are wavering opinions about the young queen. Sympathizers point to the fact that young Antoine, as she was called in her native Austria, was nothing more than a bargaining chip for her mother. When she was only ten years old, her mother arranged for her to wed Louis-Auguste, a carefully orchestrated union that would join the Austrian Hapsburgs and the French Bourbons. But detractors argue that while she had very little say in the conditions of her life, she certainly could have lived her days at court in a fashion more befitting the queen of a nation on the cusp of revolution.

While there's no point in deliberating her virtue or vices, we can delight in being voyeurs in the opulent court at Versailles, the scene of many Marie Antoinette scandals. We begin with the oft-quoted dismissal of her hungry subjects.

➤ 5. "Let Them Eat Cake!"

As famous as she is for having proclaimed, "Let them eat cake," when she heard that the peasants were starving from the dearth of bread, Marie Antoinette actually never said it.

The young queen was known to be quite tender-hearted, in contrast to her less flattering attributes as a spendthrift and wild reveler. There are accounts of her administering aid to a peasant who'd been gored by a wild animal, as well as taking in an orphaned boy. Besides accounts like these that attest to her kind and generous nature, straightforward facts disprove her utterance of this scandalous remark.

The expression comes from Jean-Jacques Rousseau's *Confessions*, a treatise penned in the late eighteenth century. When the book was first published in 1782, Marie Antoinette was ten years old and under her mother's care in Austria. There's a possibility that Rousseau turned the phrase himself; other historians think it may have been uttered by Maria Theresa. Maria Theresa was a noblewoman of Spanish descent who wed Louis XIV, the grandfather of Marie Antoinette's husband, Louis XVI.

And the expression isn't as callous as it may sound. From an economical standpoint, it was a perfectly logical thing to say. What Rousseau or Maria Theresa actually said— whatever the case may be—is "*qu'ils mangent de la brioche.*" This doesn't mean "let them eat cake;" it means "let them eat an egg-based bread." The type of bread to which the speaker referred is a more luxe loaf than the typical flour-and-water bread of the Parisian pauper. A French law mandated that bakers sell their brioche at the same price as their inexpensive bread if this supply ran out. Later on, the law would be the downfall of the hungry lower classes when bakers responded by baking very short supplies of bread to save themselves from economic ruin.

Marie Antoinette had plenty of enemies in Paris, and it was easy to fabricate stories about the queen's spendthrift habits. Very likely, someone attributed this line to the wrong royal and the tale seemed true enough to stick.

LET THEM ADMIRE MY HAIR

On June 1, 1961, French President Charles de Gaulle held a state dinner at the Palace of Versailles in honor of U.S. President John F. Kennedy. For the occasion, First Lady Jackie Kennedy wore a custom hairdo created for her by hairdresser Alexandre de Paris. Shaped like the French pastry bread, he dubbed it a "brioche." American and French women strived to emulate the style. Like Marie Antoinette, Jackie was a stylish woman who was often criticized for her extravagant taste in clothes and accessories.

4. The Diamond Necklace Affair

Like most good scandals, this one involves a smattering of

diamonds, a prostitute, and forged correspondence. We'll begin with the diamonds.

Jewelers Böhmer and Bassenge nearly went broke creating a necklace that they presumed King Louis XV would buy for his mistress, Madame du Barry. The stunner weighed in at 2,800 carats, and the jewelers thought it would fetch 1.6 million livres, roughly equivalent to 100 million U.S. dollars on today's market. Unfortunately for Böhmer and Bassenge (and Madame du Barry), the king died before he could purchase it.

The jewelers hoped that the new king, Louis XVI, might agree to buy the necklace for his queen, Marie Antoinette. But despite whatever frivolous reputation she may have acquired later in her reign, Marie Antoinette made a patriotic, sentient decision to discourage Louis from purchasing the necklace. She reasoned that he'd be better off putting the money toward France's navy.

The necklace languished in the jewelers' possession until a desperate, enterprising woman named Jeanne de Saint-Remy (Countess de Valois de la Motte) devised a plot to pull herself out of debt by acquiring the necklace and selling it for parts. The countess appealed to Cardinal de Rohan, who was rather unpopular at court. From 1772 to 1774, he'd served as the French ambassador to Vienna, where he became a quick enemy of Marie Antoinette's mother—and of Marie Antoinette herself. The countess told the cardinal that Marie Antoinette desperately wanted the diamond necklace, but that she didn't dare ask Louis for it. The countess slyly suggested that if Cardinal de Rohan could find a way to procure it for Marie Antoinette, his good reputation would be restored at court.

The countess had her lover, Rétaux de Villette, write letters in Marie Antoinette's hand and sent them to the cardinal, asking him to buy the necklace. The countess even paid a prostitute who looked like the queen to have a secret tête-à-tête with the cardinal in the Versailles gardens one night. At last, the cardinal wrangled the diamonds from Böhmer and Bassenge on credit. The jewelers presented the necklace to the queen's footman for delivery—only the footman was Rétaux in disguise. He seized the necklace and headed to London.

When his first payment was due, Cardinal de Rohan couldn't cough up the amount. The jewelers demanded money from Marie Antoinette, who had no knowledge of the necklace. By then, the necklace had been sold. A furious Louis had the cardinal arrested; later, he was acquitted of all charges and exiled. The scheming mastermind (the countess) was imprisoned but broke free and took up residence in England. There, she spread propaganda about the queen—though she needn't have bothered.

Marie Antoinette's reputation (already hanging tenuously in the balance) was ruined. The scandal confirmed that she was, indeed, "Madame Déficit." The diamond necklace affair would be one of the final straws before the French Revolution and Marie Antoinette's death sentence.

But before her head rolled, the good times did. Next, we'll peek into her boudoir and investigate her affair with a Swedish soldier.

➤ 3. The Deed with the Swede

Marie Antoinette met the Swedish soldier Hans Axel von Fersen in January 1774 at a ball in Paris. At the time, she was still the dauphine (not yet the queen), and Fersen's military career had just begun. Like many women before and after her, Marie Antoinette was instantly attracted to Fersen, who was handsome, solemn, and chivalrous. She invited him to Versailles, and he became known as one of her favorite guests. Fersen returned Marie Antoinette's affections but couldn't offer constancy. His military career blossomed into a diplomatic post and took him to England for several years and then to the American colonies, where he fought with the colonists on behalf of France.

When Louis officially became king, he gave Marie Antoinette the Petit Trianon, a three-story "pleasure house" tucked away on the vast grounds of Versailles. The house had been under construction from 1762–1768, intended for Madame de Pompadour, a mistress of Louis XV. Marie Antoinette was delighted with her acquisition and expanded its domain to include a rustic farm and town that she called Le Hameau ("the hamlet"). Quaint as the property may have been, it cost Louis 2 million francs to build (nearly 6 million U.S. dollars in 2006).

She passed much of her time in these shrouded quarters, and members of the court considered it a great honor to be invited there. In fact, those who weren't invited to the Petit Trianon circulated rumors about the queen's debauchery and reputed love affair with her close friend the Duchesse de Polignac. Louis never slept over at the Petit Trianon, though he did visit to attend theatrical performances in which Marie Antoinette played the parts of Babet and Pierette, provincial dairymaids.

Fersen was a much more frequent visitor. He had his own apartment directly above Marie Antoinette's, and judging from the correspondence between the two of them, they had a very intimate relationship. In one series of correspondence, they wrote about the acquisition and arrangement of a stove. While they were involved, Marie Antoinette still pursued her wifely duty of creating an heir to the throne. There's really no way to tell if her children were Louis's or Fersen's. But Louis accepted the children as his own, and

Marie Antoinette and her lover were careful to avoid any unwanted pregnancies.

When Marie Antoinette and her family were imprisoned at the Tuileries during the first thrust of the French Revolution, Fersen was instrumental in plotting their escape. To help them flee, he borrowed large sums of money and even mortgaged his house, acquiring a debt he never paid back in full. Unfortunately for the royals, the party was apprehended in the town of Varennes, miles from the Austrian border.

Fersen outlived his lover by nearly twenty years. On June 20, 1810, he was beaten to death by a Stockholm mob for his suspected involvement in the Swedish crown prince's death.

In a letter he wrote to his sister, Fersen explained that he would never marry because the woman he loved was taken.

➤ 2. The Brick Wall in the Bedroom

The Marie Antoinette marriage to Louis XVI did not begin smoothly. For seven years, it was unconsummated—and that was all anyone could talk about. Well, that and the brewing revolution.

The couple wed in May 1770 when he was fifteen and she was fourteen, and the ceremony and ensuing celebration had all the trappings of a lavish royal fête. At Versailles, custom permitted the king's courtiers to accompany the newlyweds to their bedroom, where they reposed on display. The custom did little to stoke the fires of passion.

Marie Antoinette was frustrated. She was willing and able to sexually receive her husband. As a matter of fact, she lived in a state of anxiety that he would never warm to her and that she'd be sent home to Austria as an utter failure. Her mother, Maria Theresa, reminded her of this danger at every possible juncture in their correspondence. She wrote to Marie Antoinette to "lavish more caresses" on Louis. What's more, it was painfully clear to everyone that something was wrong with the couple. And more was at stake than just the young couple's physical gratification: France was waiting for Marie Antoinette to produce an heir to the throne.

News of Louis's impotence spread from the court of Versailles to the streets of Paris, where pamphlets mocking his powerlessness were distributed. The propaganda planted the seed that if Louis couldn't perform in the bedroom, he certainly couldn't perform on the throne. Louis XV watched forlornly as his grandson failed to execute his mission. The reigning king had a rapacious sexual appetite and an insatiable mistress, Madame du Barry.

Young Louis was doughy, impressionable, and more fascinated by locks, languages, and hunting than he was by his lovely young wife. Marie Antoinette explained to a friend,

"My tastes are not the same as the King's, who is only interested in hunting and his metal-working." But different tastes
or not, Maria Theresa wasn't going to take the news lying
down. She sent her son Joseph to assess the couple's damage.
He called them "two complete blunderers" and surmised
that nothing else stood in their way of consummation.

Joseph may not have been entirely correct in his analysis.
Louis had been diagnosed with a condition called phimosis
in which the foreskin of the penis is tighter than normal
and doesn't loosen upon arousal. This condition made sex
very painful. There was an operation available to correct the
condition, but Louis was reluctant to go under the knife.
Some historians think he finally acquiesced and had the
procedure, while some say he never did. Regardless, the
couple finally consummated.

Marie Antoinette and Louis later wrote to Joseph, thank-
ing him for his help. Who knows what suggestive advice he
might have whispered in their ears during a walk around the
grounds of Versailles?

However, a siren call even sweeter than her husband's voice
roused Marie Antoinette from her malaise at court: fashion.

➤ 1. The National Wardrobe

When she was a young girl in Austria, Marie Antoinette
was rather rough-and-tumble. She liked horseback riding

and hunting. But at Versailles, her tomboy tendencies were squeezed out of her with each tightening of her corset. Marie Antoinette hated being put on display and having grand ceremonies made out of everyday activities like getting dressed and eating meals.

She only needed to receive a letter from her mother to remind her of her place. Marie Antoinette was, after all, in a marriage of diplomacy. Maria Theresa couldn't stand for her daughter to fail Austria. Though she acquired the reputation of a spendthrift, Marie Antoinette wasn't always so fast and loose with her budget. Her mother rebuked Marie Antoinette for keeping a slovenly appearance, and the letters she wrote to her homesick daughter were full of reminders about wearing clean clothes and grooming her hair.

Marie Antoinette traded her unfashionable togs for the latest in French couture from the house of Rose Bertin. During Louis's reign, he incurred more than 2,000 million livres in debt by contributing reinforcements to the American Revolution; Marie built up her debt in her closet. She had nearly three hundred dresses made annually for her various social engagements at the court of Versailles, at private parties at the Petit Trianon, and on the stage of her jewel-box theater.

But it wasn't just dresses that Marie and her couturier fussed over. She had an original hairstyle commissioned—the gravity-defying pouf—and even had an exclusive fragrance made for her by Jean-Louis Fargeon (also her glovemaker). Marie Antoinette's elixir evoked the gardens and orchards at the Petit Trianon, and it was supposedly so strong a scent that it gave her away during her family's plotted escape from the Tuileries.

Her pricy parties and extensive wardrobe also had helped to earn Marie Antoinette the moniker Madame Déficit. She couldn't shake the title—not that she tried. Marie Antoinette was far removed from the revolutionary murmurs in Paris. And her ignorance ultimately culminated in her death sentence.

A BELATED GIFT

In 1783, a member of the court who was quite fond of the young queen ordered a gold pocket watch for her from the Swiss company Breguet. But Marie Antoinette never received the token of affection: she was executed thirty-four years before it was completed.

Five of the Biggest Lies in History

According to myth, a young George Washington confessed to cutting down a cherry tree by proclaiming, "I cannot tell a lie." The story is testament to how much respect Americans have for their cherished first president—and honesty in general. Unfortunately, the annals of history seem to record the stories of ten dishonest scoundrels for every honorable hero like Washington.

Supposedly, the truth can set you free. But for many, deceit holds the key to money, fame, revenge, or power, and these prove all too tempting. There's also a creative aspect to it, which the following clip explores.

In history, this has often resulted in elaborate hoaxes, perjuries, and forgeries that have had enormous ripple effects. Here, we'll touch on a few of the most colossal and significant lies in history. We've sought to include a variety of lies that influenced politics, science, and even art. As a result of these, lives were lost, life savings destroyed, legitimate research hampered, and—most of all—faith in our fellow man shattered.

Without further ado, let's delve into one of the oldest and most successful lies on record.

➤ 1. The Trojan Horse

If all is fair in love and war, this might be the most forgivable of the big lies. When the Trojan Paris absconded with Helen, wife of the Spartan king, war exploded. It had been raging for ten long years when the Trojans believed they had finally overcome the Greeks. Little did they know that the Greeks had another trick up their sleeves.

In a stroke of genius, the Greeks built an enormous wooden horse with a hollow belly in which men could hide. After the Greeks convinced their foes that this structure was a peace offering, the Trojans happily accepted it and brought the horse within their fortified city. That night, as the Trojans slept, Greeks hidden inside snuck out the trap door. Then, they proceeded to slaughter and decisively defeat the Trojans.

This was unquestionably one of the biggest and most successful tricks known to history—that is, if it's actually true. Homer mentions the occurrence in the *Iliad*, and Virgil extrapolates the story in the *Aeneid*. Evidence suggests that Troy itself existed, giving some validity to Homer's tales, and scholars have long investigated how historically accurate these details are. But unfortunately, there's no concrete proof that such a contraption ever existed or was conceived beyond the imaginings of a bard. One other possible theory behind the Trojan horse comes from historian Michael Wood, who proposes that it was merely a battering ram in the shape of a horse that infiltrated the city.

In any case, the story has won a permanent place in the Western imagination as a warning to beware enemies bearing gifts.

➤ 2. Faking a Forgery: Han van Meegeren's Vermeer Villainy

This lie resulted from a classic case of wanting to please the critics. Han van Meegeren was an artist who felt underappreciated and thought he could trick art experts into admitting his genius.

In the early twentieth century, scholars were squabbling about whether the great Vermeer had painted a series of works depicting biblical scenes. Van Meegeren pounced on the opportunity and set to work carefully forging one such disputed work, *The Disciples at Emmaus*. With tireless attention to detail, he faked the cracks and aged hardness of a centuries-old painting. He intentionally played on the confirmation bias of critics who wanted to believe that Vermeer had painted such scenes. It worked: experts hailed the painting as authentic, and van Meegeren made out like a bandit producing and selling more fake Vermeers. Greed apparently overcame his desire for praise, as he decided not to out himself.

However, van Meegeren, who was working in the 1930s and 1940s, made one major mistake. He sold a painting to a prominent member of the Nazi Party in Germany. After the war, the Allies considered him a conspirator for selling a "national treasure" to the enemy. In a curious change of events, van Meegeren had to paint for his freedom. To help prove that the painting was no national treasure, he forged another in the presence of authorities.

He escaped with a light sentence of one year in prison, but van Meegeren died of a heart attack two months after his trial.

3. Anna Anderson, aka Anastasia

With the onslaught of the Russian Revolution, the existence of a royal family was intolerable to the Bolsheviks. In 1918, they massacred the royal Romanov family—Czar Nicholas II, his wife, son, and four daughters—to ensure that no legitimate heir could later resurface and rally the public for support.

Soon, rumors floated around that certain members of the royal family had escaped and survived. As one might expect, claimants came out of the woodwork. "Anna Anderson" was the most famous. In 1920, Anderson was admitted to a hospital after attempting suicide and confessed that she was Princess Anastasia, the youngest daughter of the royal family.

She stood out from other claimants because she bore a certain resemblance to the princess and had surprising knowledge of the Russian family and life at court.

Although a few relatives and acquaintances who'd known Anastasia believed Anderson, most didn't. By 1927, an alleged former roommate of Anderson claimed that her name was Franziska Schanzkowska, not Anna and certainly not Anastasia. This didn't stop Anderson from indulging in celebrity and attempting to cash in on a royal inheritance. She ultimately lost her case in the legal proceedings that dragged on for decades, but she stuck to her story until her death in 1984. Years later, upon the discovery of what proved to be the remains of the royal family, DNA tests confirmed her to be a fake. In 2009, experts were able to finally confirm that all remains have been found and that no family member escaped execution in 1918.

➤ 4. Piltdown Man

After Charles Darwin published his revolutionary *On the Origin of Species* in 1859, scientists scrambled to find fossil evidence of extinct human ancestors. They sought these so-called "missing links" to fill in the gaps on the timeline of human evolution. When archaeologist Charles Dawson unearthed what he thought was a missing link in 1910, what he really found was one of the biggest hoaxes in history.

The discovery was the Piltdown man, pieces of a skull and jaw with molars located in the Piltdown quarry in Sussex, England. Dawson brought his discovery to prominent paleontologist Arthur Smith Woodward, who touted its authenticity to his dying day.

Although the discovery gained world renown, the lie behind Piltdown man slowly and steadily unraveled. In the ensuing decades, other major discoveries suggested that Piltdown man didn't fit in the story of human evolution. By the 1950s, tests revealed that the skull was only six hundred years old and the jaw came from an orangutan. Some knowledgeable person apparently had manipulated these pieces, including filing down and staining the teeth.

The scientific world had been duped. So who was behind the fraud? Many suspects have surfaced, including Dawson himself. Today, most signs point to Martin A.C. Hinton, a museum volunteer at the time of the discovery. A trunk bearing his initials contained bones that were stained in exactly the same way that the Piltdown fossils were. Perhaps he was out to embarrass his boss, Arthur Smith Woodward, who refused to give him a weekly salary.

➤ 5. The Big Lie: Nazi Propaganda

By the time Nazism arose in Germany in the 1930s, anti-Semitism was nothing new—not by a long shot. The Jewish people had suffered a long history of prejudice and persecution. And although the Nazis perpetuated centuries-old lies, this time those lies would have their most devastating effects. Like never before, anti-Semitism was manifested in a sweeping national policy known as "the Final Solution," which sought to eliminate Jews from the face of the Earth.

To accomplish this, Adolf Hitler and his minister of propaganda, Joseph Goebbels, launched a massive campaign to convince the German people that the Jews were their enemies. Having taken over the press, they spread lies blaming Jews for all of Germany's problems, including the loss of World War I. One outrageous lie dating back to the Middle Ages claimed that Jews engaged in the ritual killings of Christian children and used their blood in the unleavened bread eaten at Passover.

Using Jews as the scapegoat, Hitler and his cronies orchestrated what they called "the big lie." This theory states that no matter how big the lie is (or more precisely, because it's so big), people will believe it if you repeat it enough. Everyone tells small lies, Hitler reasoned, but few have the guts to tell colossal lies. Because a big lie is so unlikely, people will come to accept it.

This theory helps us understand so many of the lies throughout history. Although we've barely scratched the surface of all those lies that deserve (dis)honorable mentions, hopefully we've whetted your historical curiosity.

Five Impressive Art Heists

Not all heists are silver-screen worthy, but some stand out for their ingenuity—or bravado. So how do thieves walk away with near-priceless works?

When three men walked into the E.G. Bührle Foundation museum in Zurich, Switzerland, on February 12, 2008, the masterpieces didn't stand a chance. In broad daylight, one man pulled a gun while the other two grabbed the four paintings closest to the door. It seems to be pure luck that they grabbed the most valuable piece in the museum's collection, Paul Cézanne's *Boy in the Red Waistcoat*. The thieves got out within minutes, leaving stunned museum patrons and staffers lying facedown on the floor.

Another example is the infamous theft of Edvard Munch's *The Scream* and *Madonna* from the Munch Museum in Norway in 2004. The thieves arrived with a .357-caliber Magnum pistol in hand and left with a pair of a great Norwegian artist's masterpieces—but only after having to ask where to go to find what was on their list. Since nobody argued with their self-checkout firepower, they were pointed to the paintings and left the museum with an estimated $19 million haul. Two years later, after receiving a tip, the police found the paintings in the back of a van. From their location, it looks unlikely that the thieves got the payoff they were expecting.

Yet, despite the threat of jail time and the unmistakable (read: unsellable) fame of the stolen goods, art theft has become more common in the last couple of decades, perhaps due to a combination of underfunded security and rising art prices. The 2008 Bührle robbery also proves that security doesn't mean much when thieves are willing to use force.

Art heists are increasingly conducted at gunpoint—a brute means of ensuring that the thieves get what they came for. But the most impressive art heists are the ones in which the criminals rely on something more than physical threats. We'll look at five of those in this section, starting with one that begs an age-old question: how many thieves does it take to dig a tunnel into a museum?

➤ 1. The National Fine Arts Museum in Paraguay, 2002

In July 2002, Paraguay hosted the most valuable art exhibition in its history. Then a group of criminals broke in and stole five paintings.

As it turns out, the break-in had been in the making

for months. An unidentified man rented a store 80 feet (25 meters) from the National Fine Arts Museum in Asuncion. Authorities believe he then recruited people to help him dig a tunnel 10 feet (3 meters) underground, running from the shop to the museum. After the presumed two months it took to complete the tunnel, the thieves used it to enter the museum undetected on July 30, 2002.

The thieves left with more than a million dollars' worth of art. The stolen works included *Self Portrait* by Esteban Murillo, *The Virgin Mary and Jesus* by Gustave Courbet, and Adolphe Piot's *Landscape*. As of April 2014, the paintings were still missing.

The next heist on our list has an equally impressive plan but a happier ending.

➤ 2. The Swedish National Museum, 2000

The gang who robbed the National Museum in Sweden in December 2000 knew their stuff. A machine gun will get you the haul; a bomb will distract police; and cars with flat tires can't respond to an alarm.

Their diversionary tactics were superb. While three men were inside the museum, accomplices set off two car bombs on the opposite ends of town. Local police scattered. At the same time, other accomplices were laying spikes on the roads around the museum. While one man stood inside the museum with a gun, two others located the targeted paintings.

They were in and out within a half hour, leaving with two Renoirs, *Young Parisian* and *Conversation with the Gardener*, and a self-portrait by Rembrandt. The paintings were valued at $30 million combined. The getaway vehicle was a speedboat, possible because the museum is on the waterfront.

Despite the slickness of the heist, less than two weeks later police had arrested eight men, all of whom were convicted and served jail time. One of the accomplices was a criminal lawyer brought in to negotiate the ransom.

However, the works didn't start reappearing until several years later. During a drug raid in 2001, Swedish narcotics police stumbled upon *Conversation with the Gardener*. In 2005, Danish police recovered the Rembrandt self-portrait during an attempted sale in Copenhagen. The FBI lists *Young Parisian* as also having been recovered.

Clearly, any theft is made easier when the thieves are armed. But what about thieves who use costume-shop props?

➤ 3. The Isabella Stewart Gardner Museum, 1990

With the help of goofy fake mustaches, two men managed to steal between $200 million and $300 million in paintings from Boston's Isabella Gardner Museum. At around

1:30 a.m. on March 18, 1990, thieves knocked on the museum's door. The museum guards on duty looked out and saw what appeared to be two police officers—both with big black mustaches that they would later recall as being laughable. The mustached officers said they were there to check out a reported disturbance. The guards let them in to look around.

Within minutes, the guards found themselves bound, and the thieves spent the next hour or so gathering three Rembrandts, five Degas sketches, a Vermeer, a Manet, and a bronze eagle that topped a framed Napoleon-era banner. An alarm went off while they were tearing one of the Rembrandts from its frame, but they located the source and smashed it silent. The police never showed up because it was simply an internal alarm meant to tell guards when people were getting too close to the art. Finally, the thieves told the guards that the museum would be "hearing from" them, presumably with a ransom demand, and loaded their get-away car in two trips.

But the museum never received a ransom demand. As of 2013, the thieves are still at large, none of the works have been recovered, and the FBI continues to investigate the crime. The district attorney of Boston has even promised not to prosecute whoever returns the works. The museum has offered a $5 million reward.

While the Gardner Museum is the site of the biggest heist in history, it wasn't the heist of the biggest work of art.

AN UNEXPECTED HIDEAWAY

Many of the heists listed here remain unsolved, but some thefts have resulted in unique resolutions. The Whitworth Gallery in Manchester, England, was robbed of three masterpieces in 2003: *Tahitian Landscape* by Gauguin, *Fortification of Paris with Houses* by Van Gogh, and *Poverty* by Picasso. The theft went undetected by the museum's guards, security cameras, and alarm system. But an anonymous tip led police to a public restroom the next day, where they found all three works stashed behind a toilet in a cardboard tube.

➤ 4. The Henry Moore Foundation, 2005

If something is about 12 feet (3.6 meters) long, 6 feet (1.8 meters) tall, 6 feet (1.8 meters) wide, and weighs over 2 tons (1,814 kilograms), is it worth the trouble to steal? That's a question that three men must have asked themselves after targeting a bronze sculpture by Henry Moore, *Reclining Figure*, for a potential heist. Of course, thievery involving such massive dimensions would require the use of a construction foreman's tools. Armed with a crane-equipped Mercedes flatbed truck and a Mini Cooper, these crooks had the tools for the take.

In December 2005, the two vehicles rolled into the Henry Moore Foundation courtyard at night, loaded the hippopotamus-sized sculpture onto the flatbed truck, and drove away. The entire job took ten minutes.

Thought to be worth about $4.6 million, the sculpture may have been cut up, shipped abroad, and melted down for only about $2,300 worth of scrap metal. Charles Hill, currently a private art detective in Scotland, believes the bronze piece was stolen by a group of traveling criminals. It's likely that the metal was shipped to Rotterdam and then to China to be used for electrical parts. No arrests have been made.

HOLLYWOOD HEISTS

Criminals going for broke in a big heist is time-tested movie material. *The Thomas Crown Affair* first hit theaters in 1968, and apart from stars Steve McQueen and Faye Dunaway, the subject matter—a high-stakes, high-dollar heist with a clever twist—was what captivated audiences. Add a priceless work of art to the mix, as occurs in the 1999 *Thomas Crown Affair* remake,

Ocean's Eleven, and Entrapment, and heist flicks take on even more glitz and allure. From a film producer's perspective, bagging a Monet or a Rembrandt is valuable indeed.

➤ 5. The Louvre, 1911

In 1911, da Vinci's *Mona Lisa* was stolen from the Louvre Museum in Paris in a theft that shocked the world and brought the painting to fame. On August 20, Vincenzo Peruggia, a handyman in the museum, finished his shift and hid inside an art supply closet with two brothers, Vincenzo and Michele Lancellotti. After the museum closed, they carefully lifted the two-hundred-pound framed and glass-enclosed painting from the wall, stripped da Vinci's *Mona Lisa* out, hid the painting under a blanket, and scurried off to catch a train out of Paris. The masterpiece disappeared for two years.

Museum staff didn't know the *Mona Lisa* was missing until the next day. When they saw the empty space on the wall, they assumed the painting had been removed as part of a project to photograph the Louvre's inventory. After a frequent patron asked a guard to query the photographers for their timeline, the museum staff realized the theft and called the police, but there were no clues at the scene.

Peruggia was captured two years later. He claimed the theft was a patriotic attempt to return the painting to Italy, da Vinci's homeland. But he was caught trying to sell the painting to a dealer, who immediately called the police when he realized Peruggia was indeed in possession of the highly publicized stolen painting, which had been known as a masterpiece only in select circles of the art world before its theft.

WAIT... ISN'T THAT HANGING ON MY WALL?

In 2007, Steven Spielberg's staff called the FBI about a stolen artwork. It turns out that the famous director had unknowingly purchased a Norman Rockwell painting stolen from a Missouri museum in 1973. The FBI has allowed him to keep it until it can determine the rightful owner. In a more contentious situation, a family claimed that a Van Gogh in actress Liz Taylor's collection was, in fact, stolen from its great-grandmother by the Nazis. A court ruled in 2007 that the Nazi confiscation could not be proven and that the family had waited too long to claim the work.

Ten Terribly Bungled Crimes

In addition to art thefts, the annals of true crime are filled with other types of truly amazing heists that were carefully planned and brilliantly orchestrated. The Lufthansa heist in New York in 1978 is a great example. At $5.8 million, it surpassed even the famous Brinks job in Boston, Massachusetts, in 1950, which netted the bandits more than $2.75 million in cash and checks. Both of these heists were sensational. They captured headlines from the crime to the police investigation, through the trials and beyond. But both are peanuts compared to a couple more recent ones.

In August 2005, a group of Brazilian robbers tunneled beneath two city blocks in Fortaleza and dug their way into the bank vault from beneath. The robbers snagged $70 million. The Brazilian heist was by far the largest take ever, until February 2006, when a securities storage warehouse was relieved of its cash holdings. At least five blue-collar men—including a roofer and a postman—made off with $92 million.

It's easy to see why the public imagination is so easily captured by stories like these. But what about criminals who suffer from a reversal of fortune? Like the Indiana man who, during the commission of an armed robbery in January 2008, shot himself in the groin with his own gun, effectively ending the crime. Police blotters are full of stories of criminals who clearly didn't have a grasp on the intricacies of crime. Here we recap some terrific stories of bungled crimes in no particular order.

➤ 1. Drug Deals Gone Wrong

In August 2007, a woman in Rochelle, Georgia, successfully committed the crime of purchasing and ingesting crack cocaine. But after she split her purchase and smoked one third, she found she wasn't intoxicated. Fearing that she had been ripped off, the woman, fifty-three-year-old Juanita Marie Jones, called local police to enlist their help to "get her money back." When deputies arrived at her home, she showed her purchase to them, and they promptly arrested her for possession of crack.

➤ 2. Bank Robberies

As the old saying goes, "crime doesn't pay." Or, at least it didn't for the robbers whose stories follow.

Bank robbers of questionable intelligence have been

known to use their own deposit slips as a note in the robbery. This tradition continued in September 2007, when Forest Kelly Bissonnette, a twenty-seven-year-old Englewood, Colorado, resident, passed a note to a bank teller on the back of one of his own checks. Unlike some previous robbers, Bissonnette was clever enough to make an attempt to black out his name. He failed, however, as FBI agents were able to glean the information from the check. The man was successful in making off with around $5,000. He eventually surrendered to police.

➤ 3. Cigarettes Are Bad

A man in Phoenix, Arizona, robbed a bank in July 2007, but apparently he didn't understand the rules governing police chases. While being pursued by squad cars and helicopters, the man pulled into a convenience store and ran inside. The cashier reported that the fleeing robber told him, "Quick, pack of cigarettes. Here's twenty bucks. Give me a pack of cigarettes." The cashier gave him the cigarettes, and the man quickly left the store and drove off, with police close behind. He was caught shortly after with the pack of cigarettes still unopened.

➤ 4. Caught in the Chimney

A man who went missing in 1985 turned up in the chimney of a gift shop in Natchez, Mississippi, during renovations fifteen years later. His corpse was found by masons, and he was identified by a wallet found near him. Since the missing man had a prior history of burglary, investigators concluded that he had become caught in the chimney as he tried to crawl into the gift shop to rob it. He is believed to have injured himself, which may have led to his eventual death in the chimney.

Perhaps at this point, you're thinking that one of these crooks will get a clue. But you'd be wrong. Check out the next bungled crimes.

➤ 5. Got to Catch the Bus

Go on, the song says, take the money and run. Or walk. Or take a bus.

In Atlanta in January 2008, Channel Monae Gaskin robbed a bank branch using only a stick-up note. Gaskin was in the clear until she was outside the bank and a dye bomb exploded in the money, covering her in orange paint. Not wanting to be conspicuous, she ditched the useless money and her stained clothes in a public restroom, changing into a new outfit. Then, to get away, she went to a bus stop near the bank and waited for a bus to arrive. While waiting, Gaskin was caught and arrested by police. Surprisingly, she had successfully used the Atlanta bus system as getaway transportation after a previous robbery.

➤ 6. Assassinations Foiled

Assassination attempts are rarely amusing, especially when you consider that someone would have died if everything had gone according to plan. During the trial of South African government official Dr. Wouter Basson in 2000, details of a plot to kill African leaders living in London emerged. A South African assassin picked up the proposed murder weapon, an umbrella rigged to distribute poison through a spike in the tip. The man who gave it to him accidentally tested it out on himself as he demonstrated it. He survived, but it could have been taken as an omen. Once the plan was hatched, they found one of the two targets no longer lived in London and they couldn't keep tabs on the other. The plot was abandoned and the umbrella thrown into the Thames.

➤ 7. Background Check

It would seem logical that once you've gotten away with a crime, you should stay away from police in general. This appears to have been disproven by R.C. Gaitlin, a twenty-one-year-old, who became curious when he noticed police demonstrating their equipment to local children on a Detroit street in 1988. Gaitlin asked the officers to show him as well, and handed them his driver's license for use in the demonstration of a field background check. When the police ran Gaitlin's information, they found he had a warrant out for his arrest for his involvement in a 1986 armed robbery in St. Louis. Gaitlin was arrested by the demonstrating officers.

➤ 8. Not So Fast Food

If at first you don't succeed, try, try again, right? Unless you get caught and put in jail. At least then you'll have some time to plan your next caper.

In suburban Miami in October 2007, an unidentified man placed an order at a fast food drive-through. Upon hearing that his order would cost him $7.41, he let the cashier on the other end of the speaker know that he wouldn't be paying more than the $1.75 he had on him. After being told that wouldn't do, the man drove off, only to return to the pickup window moments later on foot. He opened the window, pulled a gun on employees, and tried unsuccessfully to retrieve his order. He settled instead for a fistful of ketchup packets, but apparently decided on the way back to his car that they weren't worthwhile. He threw them to the ground and drove off.

➤ 9. Sleeping on the Job

Staying awake during the commission of a crime seems essential to keep from bungling it. A Bosnian twenty-one-year-old burglar named Edin M. scoured through a home and managed to come up with some jewelry. Customarily, burglars leave the scene of the crime after they've scored their loot. Mr. M instead opted to have a seat on a sofa in the house. He promptly fell asleep and was discovered by the home's owner. The burglar confessed to the crime and was arrested by police.

10. Writing on the Wall

In Poland in September 2007, author Krystian Bala found himself convicted of murder. Bala had written about the sensational kidnapping, torture, and murder of a fellow Pole, Dairusz Janiszewski. The story had captured headlines in the country and had baffled police for years. Bala's novel, *Amok*, featured a plotline that bore a very strong resemblance to the murder of Janiszewski. After the book caught the police's attention, they investigated Bala and discovered that not only had he known the deceased, but he also had visited the victim the last time he was seen alive and had later sold Janiszewski's cell phone. Bala received twenty-five years.

Historical Myths and Mysteries Decoded

I n this last section, we take a look at some of the weirdest myths and mysteries in world history—and answer some questions you may not even have thought to ask! Read on to learn about mummy curses and LSD at the CIA, among other great stuff you probably never learned in history class.

Did the Ancient Greeks Get Their Ideas from the Africans?

T he sitcoms you watch on TV have their roots in classical Greek comedy. The algorithms that fuel the Internet infrastructure are based on Greek mathematics. The doctors that save lives every day first take an oath based on a treatise written by the Greek physician Hippocrates. Even the scientific method dates back to ancient Greece. We here in the modern world owe much to the advancements of the classical Greeks, that much is clear. But have you ever wondered where the Greeks got their ideas?

From 1900 to 1100 BC, a great civilization reigned over what is now present-day Greece. The Mycenaeans created works of art, established trade with other nations, and lived in great cities. And then suddenly, mysteriously, the Mycenaean culture collapsed. Greece fell into darkness.

Nomadic tribes came from the north to where a bustling, urbane civilization had once stood. Trade ceased, and Greece turned inward. For five hundred years Greece stood silent, in what historians now call the Greek Dark Ages. And then, almost overnight in historical terms, a new dawn broke over Greece. Homer created his epic poems the *Iliad* and the *Odyssey*, emphasizing honor and virtue to his new countrymen. Trade resumed, and once separate city-states united into a democratic republic. Classical Greece was born.

Where did this meteoric rise to prominence come from? Scholars attribute much of Greece's development to its internalization. For five hundred years it was peacefully allowed to redevelop itself, astoundingly without any outside threats. But the loftiest of the pursuits of the Greeks would not have been possible were it not for another nearby civilization, one that was established millennia before even Mycenae was founded. The culture was called Kemet. You know it as Egypt.

The civilization that built the Sphinx, raised the pyramids, and built the world's first library also produced the world's first physician, created geometry and astronomy, and was among the first to explore the nature of our existence. The Kemites passed their knowledge along to the Greeks. Modern people, in turn, have benefited greatly from this early education.

So what exactly did the Greeks learn from the Kemites?

➤ The Kemetic Mystery System

It's well documented that classical Greek thinkers traveled to what we now call Egypt to expand their knowledge.

When the Greek scholars Thales, Hippocrates, Pythagoras, Socrates, Plato, and others traveled to Kemet, they studied at the temple-universities Waset and Ipet Isut. Here, the Greeks were immersed in a broad curriculum that encompassed both the esoteric and the practical.

Thales was the first to go to Kemet. He was introduced to the Kemetic mystery system—the knowledge that formed the basis of the Kemites' understanding of the world, which had been developed over the previous 4,500 years. After he returned to Greece, Thales made a name for himself by accurately predicting a solar eclipse and demonstrating how to measure the distance to a ship at sea. He encouraged others to make their way to Kemet to study.

In Kemet, Hippocrates, the "father of medicine," learned of disease from the previous explorations of Imhotep, who had established diagnostic medicine 2,500 years earlier. This early Renaissance man—priest, astronomer, and physician—was described as "the first figure of a physician to stand out clearly in the mists of antiquity" by the British medical trailblazer William Osler. In Kemet, Pythagoras, the "father of mathematics," learned calculus and geometry from the Kemetic priests based on a millennia-old papyrus.

None of this is to say that the Greeks were without their own ideas. On the contrary, the Greeks appear to have formed their own interpretations of what they learned in

Kemet. Nor did the Greeks ever deny the credit due to the Kemites for their education. "Egypt was the cradle of mathematics," Aristotle wrote. Rather, they seem to have put their own spin on what they'd learned.

➤ Western History Without the Kemites

We know much of this culture—thanks to the myriad documents the Kemites left and our ability to translate them using the Rosetta Stone—including that the great Greek scholars studied at the temple-universities there. For their part, the Greeks never attempted to hide where they'd learned about mathematics, astronomy, and architecture. So why don't we learn about the contributions the Kemites made to the modern world in school today?

One explanation is that while the Greeks' view of the world was based on Kemetic teachings, their stress on reason ultimately led to the Age of Enlightenment, from which we draw our world view today. The Kemites believed that the physical and the spiritual were intertwined. The concept of Ma'at—merging science and religion, and understanding that the universe is rational—was as important as geometry.

But when the Greeks formed their interpretation, reason edged out spirituality and their view of existence was passed down to us. Plato, who was among the first to extol the advantages of reason over emotion in his *Republic*, inspired the seventeenth-century philosopher Rene Descartes. Descartes's observations concerning reason inspired the modern scientific method, which has fueled a strictly rational inquiry into our existence.

Another explanation for editing out the Kemites' contribution to history is much more sinister. While Europe and the rest of the West readily credit ancient Greece as their foundation, this credit isn't extended to Africa. "During the nineteenth century, many European writers, limited by ethnocentrism and racism, decided that black Africa could have had nothing to do with Europe's rise to greatness," writes Gloria Dickenson, professor of African-American studies at the College of New Jersey.

At a time when Western society was building itself on the labor of black African slaves, white Europeans were hardly in a position to credit their slaves' ancestors with providing the foundation of that very society.

Despite proof of the Kemites' sophistication, their contributions to world culture are still perceived to be less than those of the Greeks. In an online biography of Thales, the Greek scholar's travel to Kemet to study is mentioned, although marginalized. "Thales had traveled to Egypt to study the science of geometry. Somehow he must have refined the Egyptian methods, because when he came back to Miletus he surprised his contemporaries with his unusual mathematical abilities."

Since the Kemites have been all but excluded from history, one can't help but wonder if another culture has been kept even more in the dark. A tantalizing question emerges: Did the Kemites, like the Greeks, draw their knowledge from another source?

Was There Really a Curse on King Tutankhamen's Tomb?

On February 17, 1923, a crowd of about twenty invited guests gathered in an antechamber deep within the Valley of the Kings, an elite Egyptian city of the dead. Archaeologists and Egyptian dignitaries were there to view the unsealing of King Tutankhamen's burial chamber. While the tomb's outer rooms had already revealed a treasure trove of Egyptian art and furnishings, excavators were hoping to find something more: the undisturbed mummy of King Tut.

As Howard Carter, the expedition's chief archaeologist, cleared away the stone filling between the two rooms, the assembled audience watched in silence. After ten drawn-out minutes of work, Carter created a small opening—just large enough to peer into the chamber and see light bounce off the wall of a solid gold shrine.

While the treasure of Egypt's more prominent kings and queens had long since been looted, Tutankhamen's tomb lay protected for millennia by the debris of an ancient construction project. Although thieves had entered the tomb at least twice, they had never penetrated past the second shrine of the burial chamber.

Over the next several years, Carter would excavate the most famous cache of Egyptian treasure ever found. The burial chamber's nesting shrines, solid gold coffin, and famous placid-faced mask would soon eclipse the splendor of the antechamber and annex.

But the excavation of the young king's tomb would also become famous for more ghoulish reasons. By April 1923, only two months after the chamber's unsealing, the project's financier, George Herbert, Lord Carnarvon, had died of complications from a mosquito bite. Then his dog died. Then other people connected to the dig began to die under suspicious circumstances.

Rumors began to spread that Carnarvon and the others had stirred up the "mummy's curse," a Pharaonic hex dooming those who disturbed the rest of the dead kings and queens. An inscription supposedly carved on Tutankhamen's tomb warned that "Death will come on swift pinions to those who disturb the rest of the Pharaoh."

So is there any truth behind the curse? Can you really get sick from an ancient tomb? In this section, we'll find out if the curse had any supernatural or scientific basis.

➤ The Mummy's Curse

The European and American public, already stricken by Egyptomania, seized upon the idea of the curse. Newspapers sensationalized the deaths of people connected with the expedition or its principles. Richard Bethell, Howard Carter's assistant; Bethell's father, Lord Westbury; A.C. Mace, Carter's partner; and Lady Elizabeth Carnarvon were all victims of the so-called "revenge of the Pharaohs." Judging by the list of victims, native Egyptians were not affected by the curse.

Carter was as famous for surviving the mummy's curse (at least until his death in 1939) as he is for discovering Tutankhamen's tomb—and he hated the sensationalism that surrounded the excavation. He was deeply disturbed by the public's willingness to be taken in by superstition. Carter even tried to argue that Pharaonic curses had no place in Egyptian death rituals. Tomb inscriptions sometimes contained protective formulas—messages meant to frighten off enemies from this world or beyond—but usually just wished the dead well.

In 1933, a German Egyptologist, Professor Georg Steindorff, wrote a pamphlet on Pharaonic curses, attempting to debunk the myth while also riding on its coattails. He studied the lives and deaths of the "victims," determining that many had never been near the dig and had only tenuous connections to the principal archaeologists or financiers.

But like all good curses, that of Tutankhamen's tomb became stuck in the public's imagination. Eighty years after the tomb's discovery, the *British Medical Journal* published a scientific study of the mummy's curse. Mark R. Nelson of Monash University, Australia, examined the survival rates of forty-four Westerners identified by Carter as being in Egypt during the examination of the tomb.

Nelson assumed that because the curse was a "physical entity," it had power over only those physically present during the opening of a chamber or coffin (thus removing Lord Carnarvon's dog from the roster of victims). Nelson defined several specific dates of exposure: the February 17, 1923, opening of the third door; the February 3, 1926, opening of the sarcophagus; the October 10, 1926, opening of the coffins; and the November 11, 1926, examination of the mummy. For people who were present at more than one opening or examination, Nelson accounted for their increased exposure.

Out of forty-four identified Westerners, twenty-five were present during an opening or examination. These twenty-five lived an average of 20.8 years after exposure, while the unexposed lived 28.9 years. The mean age at death for the exposed was seventy years, compared to seventy-five for the unexposed. Nelson determined that the results proved there was no curse.

But what if scientific explanation exists for the phenomena some mistook as a curse?

➤ Could You Really Get Sick from an Ancient Tomb?

Although supernatural explanations for the mummy's curse have been discredited by careful translations of protective formulas, study of Egyptian death rituals, and even modern investigations, the myth of the curse refuses to quit. Some still believe that a scientific explanation may link Lord Carnarvon's death to Tutankhamen's tomb. The financier died from erysipelas, a bacterial infection brought on by a mosquito bite. This led to septicemia, or bacteria in the bloodstream, and pneumonia. Could exposure to toxic pathogens in the tomb have killed the already ailing man?

Carter maintained that the tomb was free from "bacillary agents," but modern studies show that respiratory-attacking bacteria are sometimes present in ancient tombs. Sarcophagi can also contain formaldehyde, hydrogen sulfide, and ammonia gas—all agents that assault the lungs. Ancient meat, vegetable, and fruit funerary offerings, not to mention preserved human bodies, can attract dangerous molds like *Aspergillus niger* and *Aspergillus flavus*, while bat droppings can grow fungus.

But regardless of the potential for nasty microorganisms, experts don't think Lord Carnarvon's death was tomb-related. He died in the excavation's off-season, the time of year when it's too hot to dig in Egypt. He had been exposed to any potential bacteria, fungus, or mold months before his illness.

Carter also maintained that the conditions of the tomb were more sanitary than most of 1920s Egypt—that essentially, Lord Carnarvon was more likely to pick up a bacterial infection in modern Cairo, where he died, than in Tutankhamen's sequestered tomb. And even if a person were to catch an infection from a tomb, it would be nearly impossible to tell whether the agents that caused the infection were, in fact, ancient.

But regardless of the tomb's bacillary contents, any ancient grave lends itself to a good ghost story.

WHAT KILLED THE KING?

The fascination with King Tutankhamen's tomb, curse, and treasure extends to his own death. What killed the ruler? A 1968 X-ray showed a hole in the mummy's cranium, leading to the popular assumption that Tutankhamen was murdered. However, modern CT scans revealed greater detail, allowing scholars to recreate his face and deflate the theory of murder by blunt force. Scientists now believe archaeologists caused the hole when they removed Tut's famous mask. The CT scan also revealed a broken leg—probably not life threatening and potentially caused by embalmers.

The otherwise healthy teenager could have been poisoned but, for now at least, Zahi Hawass, PhD, Egypt's chief archaeologist, has closed the case on the boy king. In 2010, scientists used DNA studies and CT scans to suggest that Tut, who was also inbred and sickly, died of malaria and a degenerative bone condition called avascular bone necrosis—all potentially exacerbated by a leg fracture.

Did the Dutch Really Trade Manhattan for Nutmeg?

I t's the garnish of choice for eggnog, and some say it's an aphrodisiac. Nutmeg used to be a really hot commodity—so hot that the Dutch thought it was more valuable than Manhattan.

In the 1500s and 1600s, the race was on for European powerhouses to explore and conquer the best lands, trade routes, and goods from the East. By the beginning of the seventeenth century, both the Dutch and the British had broken into the Eastern trade business and emerged as forces to be reckoned with.

Both had their eyes on the West as well, because there was money to be made off the valuable fur trade there. Although their exploits in the East and West seem to have little to do with each other, the two trading powers clashed in both places. As a result, land was swapped, fortunes reversed, and fates changed in surprising ways.

The Manhattan Deal

After the English explorer Henry Hudson fruitlessly sought

a Northeast Passage to Asia via the Arctic Ocean, the Vereenigde Oost-Indische Compagnie (VOC, or Dutch East India Company) contracted with him in 1609 to search for a Northwest Passage to Asia through North America. Hudson didn't find a Northwest Passage, but he did find Long Island, Manhattan, and a river that would later bear his name.

Hudson claimed the land for the VOC, which revved up fur trading in the area in the ensuing decades. The States General of the Netherlands formed the Dutch West India Company in 1621 to colonize the land, by this time known as New Netherland.

Peter Minuit, the VOC's director general, came to New Netherland in 1626 to broker a deal with the American Indians, who occasionally used the land to hunt and fish. In exchange for the island of Manhattan, Minuit offered the tribe a chest of beads and other trinkets worth sixty guilders. In the nineteenth century, this amount was famously estimated to be about twenty-four dollars. That seems like a raw deal for the American Indians, but many historians point out that the Dutch are the ones who got conned.

The American Indians didn't have the same sense of land ownership as the Dutch did. They didn't even live on the island, which they called "Manahachtanienk," meaning, "place where we all got drunk." The American Indians simply accepted payment for land they didn't consider theirs. And it should be noted that the Dutch offering payment at all was a sign of good faith to legitimize their claims, especially compared to the Spanish conquistadors who opted simply to take the land they wanted.

Even if each party was guilty of treating the other unfairly, the Manhattan deal can still be considered a bargain—for both sides. But the Dutch didn't keep Manhattan for long.

➤ The Fight for Nutmeg

The scramble for land in North America was tame compared to the violent power struggles in the East Indies. European powers were vying for control of the spice trade, and the valuable spice at the center of it all was nutmeg.

The Europeans valued nutmeg for more than its distinct taste. Nutmeg was considered an aphrodisiac and hallucinogen. People even wore bags of the spice around their necks as protection against the Black Plague. That sounds like superstition, but nutmeg may actually have repelled fleas that carried plague-causing bacteria. Nutmeg was so highly coveted that European traders were selling it at nearly a 6,000 percent markup.

Nutmeg is indigenous to the volcanic soils of the Banda Islands, a group of islands in Indonesia. To get their hands on nutmeg, the Portuguese annexed these islands in 1512. But in the seventeenth century, the Portuguese lost their grip on that side of the world. The VOC expelled its Portuguese rivals and subsequently attempted to enforce a monopoly on nutmeg. At first, the native Bandanese population considered the Dutch their saviors from Portuguese control. However, relations soon soured.

The Dutch thought they'd secured a monopoly when they established a treaty in 1602 with village chiefs. Yet, many Bandanese nutmeg growers continued selling to other traders. Historians speculate that the Bandanese didn't understand the terms of the Dutch agreement. What's more, the Bandanese relied on bartering nutmeg for food with nearby islands.

Regardless, the Dutch felt betrayed and responded with violence against the Bandanese. In addition to a series of skirmishes, the Dutch occasionally launched sweeping attacks that resulted in the destruction of villages, enslavement of natives, and executions of chiefs. After killing thousands of natives—most of the Bandanese population—the Dutch imported their own farmers from Holland to take charge of growing nutmeg.

The VOC's struggle to maintain a monopoly on the spice was further complicated by the British, who controlled Run (also known as Pulau Run), one of the smallest of the Banda Islands. The fight for control over this island brings us back to the other island in question: Manhattan.

➤ A City for a Spice: The Treaty of Breda

To maintain their monopoly on nutmeg, the Dutch needed to make sure they were the only ones growing it. In an effort to keep people from replanting the nutmeg they sold, the Dutch dipped it in lime, which effectively prevented it from sprouting. But this wasn't the only obstacle to overcome in their nutmeg monopoly. The British were still dabbling in the nutmeg trade from their stores on the island of Run. Though small, the island of Run was rife with nutmeg. The British East India Company (EIC) had secured a successful partnership early on with the island's leaders to trade its nutmeg.

Jan Pieterszoon Coen, the ruthless commander of the VOC, was dead set on expelling the British any way he could. Much to his chagrin, however, the VOC and EIC officials back in Europe signed a cooperation agreement in 1619. But Coen decided that if he couldn't have Run's nutmeg, then no one could. In lieu of direct violence against the British, he sneaked onto the island when the British left it undefended and burned down all the nutmeg trees. Finally, in 1666, during the Second Anglo-Dutch War, the VOC took control of Run.

Meanwhile, things weren't going so well for the Dutch in the West. Fur trade in New Netherland wasn't nearly as lucrative as nutmeg trade in the East. To make matters worse, a British fleet had succeeded in taking over New Amsterdam (the Dutch name for Manhattan) in 1664. The 1667 Treaty of Breda allowed the Dutch and British to formally settle their differences. In exchange for official control of Run, the Dutch relinquished their claims to New Amsterdam.

The British weren't very excited about the trade, and they initially tried to pawn Manhattan off for valuable sugar-producing lands in South America. As fate would have it, the Dutch didn't agree with this trade, and the British kept the island, later renaming it New York.

BRINGING NUTMEG WEST

During the Napoleonic wars of the early nineteenth century, the British invaded the Banda Islands. Taking lime-free nutmeg with them, they were able to replant these seeds in places like the Caribbean island of Grenada. Grenada is now among the leading producers of the spice, and a nutmeg is featured on the country's flag.

Could Jack the Ripper Have Been an Artist?

Being a prostitute in London, England, must have been particularly unsettling in 1888. In addition to the usual dangers that accompany such a profession, a madman—a butcher of women—was on the prowl in the fall of that year in the city's East End. At least five women were murdered by a serial killer who'd led them to believe he was merely a customer. They met their ends in a most brutal fashion, and the crimes became known as the Ripper murders.

In one case, a victim's kidney was removed and taken as a souvenir. In another, the victim's sex organs were dissected. An equally gruesome case involved an interrupted amputation in which the killer left behind a partially removed leg. The city was whipped into a frenzy by news of these horrible murders. The press called this monster "Jack the Ripper." The killer was bold, murdering his victims on the street in some cases, and leaving their eviscerated remains for any casual passerby to find.

According to popular belief, there were other victims,

including one woman whose torso was discovered beneath a tarp and her arms and legs found floating in the Thames River. The London constabulary (police department) ultimately attributed five murders, all female prostitutes, to the Ripper. These serial killings took place between August 31 and November 9, 1888, in the Whitechapel area of London. Two took place within an hour of each other on September 30. That fall, London became a place of fear.

And then, as quickly as it had begun, the killing spree stopped. Jack the Ripper withdrew into the shadowiest corner of history.

For more than a century, countless people have doggedly pursued the true identity of Jack the Ripper. These Ripperologists use historical research and analysis from the London police and Scotland Yard's nineteenth-century investigation to guide their efforts. Amateur criminologists and historians have nominated dozens of possible suspects in the case, none of whom have been definitively identified as Jack the Ripper. So the quest continues.

In 2002, popular crime-fiction novelist Patricia Cornwell advanced her own theory of Jack the Ripper's identity. She released *Portrait of a Killer: Jack the Ripper—Case Closed*, a nonfiction book in which she identifies her Ripper suspect. Let's find out why Cornwell is certain that a well-known nineteenth-century British artist was Jack the Ripper.

➤ Patricia Cornwell's Suspect

In 2002, novelist Patricia Cornwell produced a nonfiction book in which she revealed that Jack the Ripper was actually Walter Sickert. The intelligent (and reputedly egotistical) British impressionist painter was twenty-eight at the time of the Whitechapel murders. A successful artist, Sickert was known to paint and draw nudes of brutalized women. Not only did Cornwell believe that Sickert was the Ripper, but she also postulated that he took his act on the road from London to the English countryside and France. His excursions outside of London, Cornwell believes, included murdering children as well as women.

The author's investigation took on the tones of obsession. She even cut apart a Sickert painting in search of evidence. No one's sure what she expected to find inside the painting, but other Ripperologists have found his artwork suspicious as well. One moody, dark painting, titled *The Camden Town Murder*, shows a naked woman lying on a bed, perhaps dead, with a man seated on the edge of the bed, fully clothed. To Cornwell, it's tantamount to Sickert's murder confession.

Cornwell found her most tangible support by using a modern investigative technique: DNA testing. She visited Scotland Yard and examined several hundred documents and letters supposedly written by Jack the Ripper.

Cornwell and Ripperologists are aware that most (if not all) of these letters were written by people other than the murderer. Letters from people claiming to be Jack the Ripper were sent to Scotland Yard into the 1960s. (Sickert, incidentally, died in 1942.) Some of the earliest letter forgers—two of whom were women—were arrested around the time of the murders.

When the DNA test results were returned to Cornwell, she found a match. She had results from Ripper letters compared to samples taken from some of Sickert's known correspondence. She found a match among mitochondrial DNA (mtDNA) that ruled out 99 percent of the human population, but not Sickert. Mitochondrial DNA doesn't degrade as easily as nuclear DNA. This is significant, considering the Ripper letters that provided matches had been written a century before.

Patricia Cornwell isn't the only author to point to Sickert as Jack. At least two others, the first in 1970, have arrived at the same conclusion. Like Cornwell, they view Sickert's paintings as evidence of his guilt. They believe the paintings contain clues—which Sickert purposely included—to his identity as Jack the Ripper.

Some Ripperologists (including Cornwell) believe that Sickert actually used the murdered prostitutes as models for his paintings. The artist was trained under American painter James Whistler to paint only from life. So if Sickert followed Whistler's methodology, we could infer that Sickert must've seen the corpses of the women in his paintings firsthand. But there's no definitive proof that he had access to them—or that he murdered the women himself.

Sickert is said to have admitted there were clues in his paintings related to the Ripper murders. But, according to a man who claimed to be his illegitimate son, Sickert said he'd put the clues there to point to another theory of the killings—that they were part of a royal cover-up.

And then there's the theory that one of the Ripperologists' likeliest suspects was himself a Ripperologist. This ironic twist underscores the slippery slope of the investigation in the Whitechapel murders, a case that may never be closed. In addition, some holes in Cornwell's theory keep it from definitively solving the case.

➤ The Artist Is Exonerated?

As soon as Patricia Cornwell's book naming Walter Sickert as Jack the Ripper was published, dedicated Ripperologists set about poking holes in her theory and methods. One critic, a curator of Sickert works at the Royal Academy in London, called her "monstrously stupid" for destroying a Sickert painting in the name of research.

Most other criticism has been leveled at Cornwell's

conclusion. Chief among this criticism from Ripperologists is her use of mitochondrial DNA.

We receive our mtDNA from our mother's lineage only, which makes it less accurate in identifying our cells than the unique combination of DNA found in our cells' nuclei. While Cornwell's mtDNA sample ruled out 99 percent of the population, this still left nearly fifty thousand London residents, in addition to Sickert, who may have produced an mtDNA match.

Ripperologists critical of Cornwell point out that while Walter Sickert may have sent the Ripper letters that provided this DNA match, this doesn't prove he was also the killer. Sickert was well known for his prolific letter writing to the editors of local newspapers. He was also very interested in the Ripper murders. So it's perhaps less of a stretch to assume that Sickert wrote the letter as a bizarre prank than to assume that because he wrote the letters, he was the Ripper.

The use of paintings as evidence is also called into question by some Ripperologists. As anyone interested in art knows, paintings are open to interpretation by the observer. But Ripperology puts little stock in art appreciation. While Sickert's paintings can be taken to depict dead women, the women pictured could also be sleeping or resting. The work that's most often cited as evidence of the painter's guilt is *The Camden Town Murder*. But as Ripperologist Wolf Vanderlinden points out, Sickert gave this painting an alternate title: *What Shall We Do for Rent?* Under this other title, the menace in the painting is replaced by a sense of desperation and uncertainty. Murderer and victim become simply a couple who've fallen on hard times.

It's possible that Sickert did use the murdered women as subjects for his paintings. It's also possible that the artist did so as an attempt at grisly humor or simply out of interest in the Ripper case—art imitating life. Cornwell's assertion that Sickert only painted things he saw in real life is undermined by evidence that Sickert did, in fact, paint from photographs on occasion—especially later in life. And when the artist produced his most "confessional" paintings around 1905, a book containing photos of the Whitechapel murder victims had already been published for six years.

Ultimately, there are too few clues to definitively identify Walter Sickert or any of the other suspects as Jack the Ripper. While Patricia Cornwell is satisfied with her closed case, the century-old manhunt continues for Ripperologists pursuing their own theories.

Who Was Rosie the Riveter?

With her stoic expression and flexed bicep, Rosie the Riveter really can do it. And for the women of the World War II generation, that meant anything from riveting to welding. But eventually even Rosie's pert, polka-dotted headscarf scraped the glass ceiling.

As American men departed for the war front in World War II, they left behind vitally important factory, war production plant, and civil service jobs. These were booming industries, thanks to increased demand caused by the war, or positions necessary for daily life, like post office workers. It was quite a predicament, and the U.S. government turned to the War Advertising Council, which implemented a massive national campaign to usher women into the workplace. Known as the Women in War Jobs campaign, it is considered even today to be the advertising industry's most successful "recruitment" campaign in the United States.

The propaganda campaign used a series of persuasive patriotic posters and messages featuring different versions of the now-legendary icon Rosie the Riveter. One version of Rosie painted by *Saturday Evening Post* artist Norman Rockwell depicts the antithesis of prewar femininity: a muscular woman in factory garb, brandishing a riveting machine and her lunch box.

The campaign targeted several groups of women. First, women already in the workplace (particularly minority women and those who held low-paying positions) were encouraged to upgrade to factory jobs with better wages. Next, girls barely out of high school were recruited. After it became obvious that still more workers were necessary, the campaign went after married women with children who didn't really need—or even want—to work. Several persuasive messages permeated the campaign, especially the importance of patriotism and the idea that the war would end sooner if women at home filled the shoes of absent male workers. Fear propaganda also insisted that more soldiers would perish and women would be considered "slackers" if they didn't step up to the task.

These efforts were wildly successful. By 1945, more than eighteen million women were in the workforce—up from twelve million in 1940. Many of these women were employed in traditionally male-dominated roles, such as aerodynamic engineers, railroad workers, streetcar drivers, and lumber and steel mill employees. Despite the fact that the women were doing the same jobs as their absent male counterparts, they earned roughly 65 percent less. Women in the workplace also had to contend with the negative attitudes of male coworkers, exclusion from higher-ranking positions, and other glass ceiling effects.

So how does Rosie the Riveter figure into all of this?

➤ "We Can Do It": The Real Rosie the Riveters

First things first: What is a "riveter," anyway? A riveter is someone who operates a riveting gun, a necessary tool in the manufacturing industry. Many of the women who were inspired to join the work force by Rosie the Riveter actually did very little (if any) riveting, simply because their jobs didn't require it. In fact, the number of women who filled manufacturing roles never exceeded 10 percent of the overall women's working class, which numbered some nineteen million.

The Rosie phenomenon came about following the beginning of United States involvement in World War II in 1941. A song titled "Rosie the Riveter," written by John Jacob Loeb and Redd Evans, was released in the early months of 1943. The lyrics described exactly the type of role the government was hoping women would fill during wartime: "She's a part of the assembly line, she's making history, working for victory, Rosie the Riveter."

On May 29, 1943, Rockwell's depiction of Rosie

appeared on the cover of the *Saturday Evening Post*. At the time, Rockwell had a reputation as the most popular illustrator in the country, so his cover reached a massive audience, bringing Rosie's unique and groundbreaking image to the forefront of attention. Rockwell sought nineteen-year-old Mary Doyle to serve as a model for Rosie, although he made some drastic changes to her natural appearance by adding a muscular physique.

But while Rockwell's version of Rosie may have been the most popular of its era, another version of Rosie—the jaunty girl flexing her bicep and sporting a polka-dotted scarf on her head—endures today. This Rosie was created in 1942 by an artist named J. Howard Miller. Miller was contracted by an advertising agency to create the image for Westinghouse Electric and Manufacturing Company. The poster was intended for private use in Westinghouse factories from February 15 to 28, 1932, and the public didn't really discover it until the 1980s. Now, the image is one of the top ten most frequently requested images from the National Archives.

Many people continue to interpret Rosie as a feminist icon, but revisionist historians stress that she was not. She was appropriated by different parties for a similar reason: to beckon women into the workplace. Unfortunately for many women who had grown accustomed to working and the financial independence that resulted from their jobs, Rosie's purpose was extinguished at the end of the war. Although employers had grown to accept women in the workplace, the return of the soldiers to the home front forced them to admit that their recently adopted female staff had been only temporary—for the most part.

Those women who continued to work outside their homes were pressured to take more socially accepted and lower-paying jobs, like secretarial positions. Although these gender disparities took hold once again, it was too late to close the floodgates. Before long, the daughters of these women began to chip away at archaic ideas, making way for the women of today to seek higher education and excel in professional roles. While the need for Rosie propaganda may no longer be necessary, her we-can-do-it attitude has left an imprint in history.

Did the CIA Test LSD on Unsuspecting Americans?

A bad LSD trip can drive a person to suicide. So what would have inspired the Central Intelligence Agency (CIA) to use American citizens as guinea pigs for its drug research?

You, like any other sane person, perceive a concrete world, one that's generally calm and unmenacing. Everyday objects remain still and solid and don't tend to melt into their surroundings. Most likely, no one is out to get you; strangers aren't actually actors in an elaborate and nefarious ruse at which you are the uninformed center. There may or may not be a God; the secrets of the universe remain sequestered from you.

All of this changes with LSD. The potent hallucinogen lysergic acid diethylamide can temporarily occupy the psyche of a person who ingests it. Because of its potency and ability to unlock the "doors of perception," as author Aldous Huxley put it, LSD can be psychically violent. It can hijack the user's mind, gently revealing life's latent truths, or it can turn bully, reducing the user to a state of abject fear.

Psychologist Timothy Leary proposed that the latter, a bad trip, could be prevented by mindset and setting. The mind-set of the user and the atmosphere where the trip takes place are of the utmost importance, in Leary's view.

This makes dosing an unsuspecting person with it—especially one who isn't already experienced with LSD's properties—a particularly ghastly act. A person unacquainted with LSD and unaware he or she'd been given it could be brought to the edge of mental breakdown.

So one could consider the CIA downright cruel for administering LSD to an unknown number of unsuspecting Americans during the 1950s and 1960s. The agency conducted clandestine experiments on college students, drug addicts, veterans, soldiers, sailors, johns, and mental patients, as well as at least one young mother and a jazz singer. For a time, the drug was so prevalent in the CIA that agents dosed one another for fun. And for a punch line, the heyday of 1960s counterculture—including its subversion of the establishment—was preceded and directly created by the CIA's acid tests.

➤ Acid in the Hands of the CIA: MKULTRA

In 1951, the CIA received word from a military envoy that the Swiss drug company Sandoz Pharmaceuticals had one hundred million doses of LSD available to anyone who cared to purchase them. This "anyone" included the Russians—people who, in the minds of the U.S. military and intelligence communities, were shady, powerful, and unscrupulous. In the hands of the Soviet Union, they thought, entire U.S. cities could be driven mad or made to revolt against the U.S. government from a water supply spiked with LSD.

The Russians, the CIA knew, were engaged in tests to find ways of undermining the behavior and personalities of regular people. They wanted to create a truth serum or learn to program everyday individuals to become unwitting and involuntary assassins. So, too, did the Americans.

When the Sandoz supply became known, the United States moved to take it off the market. With the LSD in their possession, military researchers and the CIA began conducting their own experiments.

In the 1970s, Congress held inquiries into the clandestine operation known as MKULTRA, the code name for a CIA umbrella operation covering 149 subprojects. Most of these were involved with exploring new methods of chemical and psychological warfare. The CIA maintained its standard silence—files had been destroyed, new directors had no knowledge of old projects—until the skeleton in the CIA's closet that was MKULTRA emerged entirely. A Freedom of Information Act request filed by a journalist turned up several boxes of materials that escaped destruction, and information on 149 MKULTRA subprojects was unearthed. These projects ranged from learning to deliver poisons using magicians' sleight of hand to electroshock therapy as a means of making an unwilling subject talk.

Sidney Gottlieb, PhD, a clubfooted, stuttering scientist with a penchant for dancing, ran the technical division for the CIA. George Hunter White, a former Army Office of Strategic Services (the predecessor of the CIA) officer who'd reputedly killed a Chinese spy with his bare hands in Calcutta, directly oversaw the undercover acid tests for Gottlieb. Ike Feldman, a narcotics agent who posed comfortably as a pimp and racketeer, did much of the leg work at White's direction. Separately, but especially together, these three men filled out every inch of the shady public image of CIA operatives. They were the spooks of pulp fiction realized.

Most of the MKULTRA experiments were conducted under the scientific method with informed, willing test subjects at universities, CIA labs, and independent research facilities. Some of these tests fell outside the bounds of acceptable protocol. One study lured heroin addicts to participate as test subjects by paying them in heroin. Another studied the effects of LSD on black inmates in a prison. The experiments carried out by White and Feldman at Gottlieb's behest were less scientific. These resembled torture or a party, depending on how the subject reacted to the acid.

➤ CIA LSD Experiments

George Hunter White was already a legend in the law enforcement community by the time he was recruited by the CIA to carry out Gottlieb's experiments. He'd made a name for himself by working undercover as a heroin trafficker and taking down a syndicate of Chinese opium dealers. White was a little too good at his job; he was excommunicated from New York after digging up political dirt on the governor. He was a swinger, whose sexual proclivities tended toward the kinky. By all accounts, White was crazy, reckless, and the perfect man to get the job done when the job took nerve, heartlessness, and a complete disregard of established laws and social norms.

At first it was White who carried out Gottlieb's tests. White and his ostensibly informed wife held parties at their New York apartment where White furnished his guests with LSD-laced martinis. As the drug took hold, he observed its effects on the unwitting participants, making notes on their reactions. In some instances, the effects included giddiness and euphoria; others were darker, with the subjects realizing something was terribly wrong and reacting badly. White noted this type of reaction as "the horrors."

Eventually, the experiments were moved from White's apartment to a CIA-funded safe house in San Francisco dubbed "the pad." It was here that White recruited Ike

Feldman. In his guise as pimp, the cop collected prostitutes and paid them to bring back customers to the pad and surreptitiously administer LSD in their drinks. Throughout, George White sat quietly behind a two-way mirror, drinking martinis, watching the ignorant test subjects trip, and taking notes on their reactions.

Unlike the legitimate experiments held in research facilities, the covert experimenters failed to keep an appropriate and objective distance from their tests. Instead, the CIA higher-ups determined it would be best for their operatives to try LSD themselves, an effort to prepare them in the event they should be slipped the drug by Soviet agents. They would be better equipped to handle the bent version of reality.

This official decision either led to or justified a culture of acid users in the CIA in the 1950s; it's unclear which came first. Either way, in the middle of the twentieth century, a significant number of CIA operatives knew what it meant to trip on acid. The "beauty" of LSD wasn't experienced by all involved in the clandestine tests, however. At least one person is believed to have died as an indirect result of what can only be described as a truly bad trip, and others' lives were ruined by the CIA's surreptitious dosing.

ONE FLEW OVER THE LSD TEST

There was one last footnote to the MKULTRA LSD sub-project, one unintended and unforeseen side effect. Ken Kesey, author of *One Flew Over the Cuckoo's Nest*, and arguably the founder of the hippie movement of the 1960s, was a willing participant in a separate, legitimate MKULTRA LSD experiment. Kesey brought his experience with acid to his friends, and by extension, whole generations of American youth were introduced to LSD.

On the record, MKULTRA was disbanded in the early 1970s, just another agency secret. Once information about MKULTRA emerged, it confirmed any "paranoid" or "delusional" fears of just what the U.S. government is capable of when it believes it's threatened.

The men involved escaped punishment. George White retired in 1965, opting for a life of terrorizing his neighbors in Stinson Beach, California, by driving his Jeep across their front lawns. Ike Feldman retired later, forced out of a later job at the Drug Enforcement Administration. Gottlieb retired to spend his remaining days volunteering with dying AIDS and cancer patients, working, he said, "on the side of the angels instead of the devils."

QUIZ: THE ULTIMATE STUFF YOU MISSED IN HISTORY CLASS QUIZ

N ow that you've reached the end of this crash course in the coolest and weirdest history, it's time to test what you've learned! Good luck and have fun. Check your answers in the back of the book on page 231.

1. **True or False: More humans live in caves today than at any other time in human history.**

    a. True

    b. False

2. **Which of the following was NOT part of the Vikings' gear?**

    a. A wooden shield

    b. A horned helmet

    c. A padded leather shirt or iron breastplate

3. **How long is the Great Wall of China?**

    a.   1,500 miles

    b.   4,163 miles

    c.   15,463 miles

    d.   13,170 miles

4. **Which of the following types of weapons did ninja use?**

    a.   Ninja throwing stars

    b.   Brass knuckles

    c.   Small, sharp tacks

    d.   All of the above

5. **Why were Aboriginal children in the 1900s called the "Stolen Generation"?**

    a.   Their parents stole their childhood by forcing them to grow up too fast.

    b.   White Australians took Aboriginal children from their homes and raised them as white children.

    c.   They were particularly susceptible to stealing from others.

    d.   White Australians stole land, money, and goods from the Aboriginal parents of these children.

6. **The Scavenger's Daughter was a vicious medieval torture device that was**

   a. a hoop of iron used to dislocate the spine and crack bones.

   b. an upright sarcophagus with spikes on the inner surfaces used to pierce vital organs.

   c. a metal claw that shredded a woman's breast.

   d. a hollow brass statue in which the victim was trapped and burned alive.

7. **Which of the following was NOT a Prohibition term for alcohol?**

   a. Hooch

   b. Giggle water

   c. Rum runner

   d. Moonshine

8. **True or False: Toxic pathogens killed Lord Carnavon, the head of the accursed excavation of King Tut's tomb.**

   a. True

   b. False

9. **What is a "riveter"?**

    a. Someone who gives riveting speeches

    b. A device used in railroad work

    c. A word for a symbol or icon that represents feminist ideals

    d. A person who operates a riveting gun (a manufacturing tool)

10. **True or False: CIA agents used to secretly spike fellow agents' drinks with LSD for work purposes.**

    a. True

    b. False

Answers to the Quizzes

➤ Could You Fit in as a Musketeer?

1. The action in the novel *The Three Musketeers* takes place in what era?

   Answer: B. The story is set in the 1620s during the reign of French King Louis XIII.

2. Who was Alexandre Dumas?

   Answer: B. Dumas wrote the novel *The Three Musketeers* in the 1840s.

3. At the beginning of the novel *The Three Musketeers*, who is d'Artagnan?

   Answer: C. D'Artagnan arrives in Paris from Gascony with the dream of becoming a musketeer.

4. **What was the motto of the three musketeers in the novel?**

    Answer: B. All for one and one for all was the musketeers' motto.

5. **The original musket was a heavy firearm invented in which country?**

    Answer: C. The original musket, known locally as a moschetto, was invented in Spain.

6. **Which of the following was NOT a nougat flavor in the original 3 Musketeers candy bar?**

    Answer: B. The original three nougat flavors were strawberry, vanilla, and chocolate.

7. **In duels, the musketeers relied mainly on which weapon?**

    Answer: A. The sword or rapier was the traditional dueling weapon at the time.

8. **What was a Huguenot?**

    Answer: B. A Huguenot was a French Protestant.

9. True or False: The quintessential musketeer's uniform included a blue tunic trimmed with gold lace and a three-cornered hat.

    Answer: B. Certainly the blue tunic with gold lace was a must-have fashion statement for a musketeer, but the three-cornered hat was not. It was utilized by Minutemen in the American Revolution.

10. True or False: The Musketeers of the Guard still exist today as a ceremonial unit in France.

     Answer: B. The Musketeers were disbanded completely in 1816.

➤ The Ultimate Witches Quiz

1. The word "pagan" comes from the Latin *pagini*, which means what?

    Answer: B. The connotations of "pagan" didn't start off negatively. In fact, the word comes from the Latin word meaning "home dweller" or "country person."

2. **During the Salem witch trials in 1692, the two girls who accused women of practicing witchcraft may have suffered from what condition?**

Answer: C. The two girls who blamed their convulsions and painful sensations of being pinched and bitten on witchcraft may have suffered from clinical hysteria. Twenty people were executed as a result of their claims.

3. **How long did witch hunts last in Europe?**

Answer: C. The Middle Ages weren't a good time for witches in Europe. Witch hunts lasted in Europe and European colonies from the 1450s to the 1750s.

4. **What is a witch's broomstick used for?**

Answer: B. Witches don't actually fly on brooms, although many do have them. They're used to purify an area of lingering energies (similar to the use of burning sage) before "casting a circle." Circles are cast before any ritual.

5. **The Wiccan religion, which draws on ancient pagan beliefs and rituals, was created when?**

    Answer: C. Wicca, a modern pagan religion that worships the Earth and nature, was established in Britain in the 1940s and '50s by Gerald Gardner, who defined witchcraft as a positive and life-affirming religion. The central Wiccan theme is, "If it does no harm, do your own will."

6. **True or False: A "warlock" is a male witch.**

    Answer: B. Men are also called witches, not warlocks. The word warlock actually means "oath breaker" and dates back to the witch hunts: it was used to refer to those who betrayed other witches, and in the witching world it still has a bad connotation.

7. **The magic of modern witchcraft is technically referred to as what?**

    Answer: A. Modern witches refer to their craft as magick, to differentiate it from magicians' illusion work.

8. **If Wiccans perform magick intended to harm someone else, what will supposedly happen?**

Answer: C. Since Wiccans are taught to do no harm, ill-intended magick will be returned to them threefold. Wiccan magick is intended for personal change only.

➤ The Ultimate Stuff You Missed in History Class Quiz

1. **True or False: More humans live in caves today than at any other time in human history.**

Answer: A. The era that most people think of when they talk about "cavemen" is the Paleolithic Era, sometimes referred to as the Stone Age. It extends from more than two million years ago until between forty thousand and ten thousand years ago (depending on who you ask). Ironically, there are probably more humans permanently living in caves today than at any time in human history.

2.   **Which of the following was NOT part of the Vikings' gear?**

Answer: B. One thing Vikings almost certainly did not wear on their heads was a horned helmet. Such a device would be impractical in battle, with excess weight poorly distributed, offering no real protective value.

3.   **How long is the Great Wall of China?**

Answer: D. In 2012, a five-year-long study conducted by two Chinese government organizations announced the wall's length from east to west as a whopping 13,170 miles long!

4.   **Which of the following types of weapons did ninja use?**

Answer: D. All of these were weapons employed by ninja to deter attackers or pursuers or to carry out assassinations. Ninja also used short swords or knives, roped weapons, smoke bombs, and other gear.

5. **Why were Aboriginal children in the 1900s called the "Stolen Generation"?**

Answer: B. Beginning in 1910, non-indigenous Australians began to take Aboriginal children from their homes and families. These children, known as the Stolen Generation, were either given to white families—to be raised as white children—or to institutions and orphanages where they were forced to assimilate to white society. Between 1910 and 1970, when the practice stopped, over one hundred thousand children had been separated from their families and culture.

6. **The Scavenger's Daughter was a vicious medieval torture device that was:**

Answer: A. The Scavenger's Daughter was a torture device commonly used to crack bones and dislocate the spine. Made of a hoop of iron with a hinge, it trapped its victims and slowly crushed them with each tightening of the hinge.

7.   **Which of the following was NOT a Prohibition term for alcohol?**

Answer: C. A rum runner was a person who smuggled alcohol during Prohibition.

8.   **True or False: Toxic pathogens killed Lord Carnavon, the head of the accursed excavation of King Tut's tomb.**

Answer: B. Regardless of the potential for contact with nasty microorganisms when opening a tomb, experts don't think Lord Carnarvon's death was tomb-related. He died in the excavation's off-season, the time of year when it's too hot to dig in Egypt. He had been exposed to any potential bacteria, fungus, or mold months before his fatal illness.

9.   **What is a "riveter"?**

Answer: D. A riveter is someone who operates a riveting gun, a necessary tool in the manufacturing industry.

10. True or False: CIA agents used to secretly spike fellow agents' drinks with LSD for work purposes.

Answer: A. In the 1950s and '60s, CIA higher-ups determined it would be best for their operatives to try LSD themselves, to prepare them in the event they should be slipped the drug by Soviet agents. They would be better equipped to handle the bent version of reality. CIA agents took to slipping their own colleagues drugs without them knowing.

Sources

➤ The Dawn of Humanity: How Cave Dwellers Work

Agence France-Presse. "Palestinian Cave Dwellers Defy Creeping Occupation." September 26, 2007. www.lebanonwire.com /0709MLN/07092618AF.asp.

Aujoulat, Norbert. *Lascaux: Movement, Space and Time*. New York: Abrams, 2005.

BBC. "Sawney Bean: Scotland's Hannibal Lecter." February 2004. Accessed July 1, 2008. www.bbc.co.uk/legacies/myths_legends /scotland/s_sw/article_2.shtml.

Constable, Nick. *Atlas of Archeology*. London: Mercury Books, 2008.

Lynch, John and Louise Barrett. *Walking with Cavemen: Eye-to-Eye with Your Ancestors*. London: Headline Publishing Group, 2003.

Price, Matthew. "Underground Art." *Washington Post*, December 17, 2006. Accessed July 1, 2008. www.washingtonpost.com/wp-dyn /content/article/2006/12/14/AR2006121401459.html.

Tattersall, Ian. *The Last Neanderthal: The Rise, Success, and Mysterious Extinction of Our Closest Human Relatives*. New York: Basic Books, 1999.

Viegas, Jennifer. "Neanderthals and Humans Shared Cave." Discovery News. May 3, 2005. Accessed July 1, 2008. www.abc.net.au /science/articles/2005/05/03/1358479.htm.

| | | | |

➤ How the Vikings Worked

Cohat, Yves. *The Vikings: Lord of the Seas*. New York: Abrams, 1992.

Fitzhugh, William. "Early Encounters with a 'New' Land: Vikings and Englishman in the North American Arctic." In *Unlocking the Past: Celebrating Historical Archaeology in North America*, edited by Lu Ann De Cunzo and John H. Jameson, 53–61. Gainesville, FL: University Press of Florida, 2005.

Haywood, John. *Atlas of World History*. New York: MetroBooks, 2000.

Haywood, John. *Encyclopaedia of the Viking Age*. London: Thames & Hudson, 2000.

Hurstwic. "Viking Age Arms and Armor: Viking Helmets." Accessed April 14, 2008. www.hurstwic.org/history/articles/manufacturing /text/viking_helmets.htm.

MacShamhrain, Ailbhe. *The Vikings: An Illustrated History*. Dublin: Wolfhound Press, 2003.

Wolf, Kirsten. *Daily Life of the Vikings*. New York: Greenwood Press, 2004.

| | | | |

➤ The Impenetrable Fortress: How the Great Wall of China Works

BBC News. "China to Measure the Great Wall." February 11, 2007. news.bbc.co.uk/2/hi/asia-pacific/6352239.stm.

BBC News. "Party Ban at China's Great Wall." October 25, 2006. news .bbc.co.uk/2/hi/asia-pacific/6083044.stm.

Bowden, Charles. "Our Wall." *National Geographic Magazine*, May 2007. ngm.nationalgeographic.com/print/2007/05/us-mexican -border/bowden-text.

China Highlights. "Great Wall of China." Accessed July 23, 2007. www .chinahighlights.com/greatwall/.

Hessler, Peter. "Chasing the Wall." *National Geographic Magazine*, January

2003.   ngm.nationalgeographic.com/print/features/world/asia/china/great-wall-text.

History.com. "Life after People: Landmarks." Accessed July 23, 2008.

History.com. "Seven Ancient Wonders of the World." Accessed July 23, 2008.   www.history.com/minisite.do?content_type=Minisite_Generic&content_type_id=54820&display_order=2&sub_display_order=2&mini_id=54814.

Mooney, Paul. "Great Wall of China Overrun, Damaged, Disneyfied." National Geographic News. May 15, 2007. news.national geographic.com/news/2007/05/070515-china-neglect.html.

National Geographic.com. "The Great Wall Zoom In." 2003. Accessed July 28, 2008. ngm.nationalgeographic.com/ngm/0301/feature 1/zoom1.html.

National Geographic Daily News. "New 7 Wonders vs. Ancient 7 Wonders." Accessed July 23, 2008. news.nationalgeographic.com/news/2007/07/photogalleries/seven-wonders/photo2.html.

National Geographic News Photo Gallery. "New 7 Wonders vs. Ancient 7 Wonders." Accessed July 23, 2008. news.nationalgeographic.com/news/2007/07/photogalleries/seven-wonders/photo2.html.

National Geographic Traveler. "China Photo Gallery." 2008. travel.nationalgeographic.com/travel/countries/china-cities-photos/.

NewsGD.com. "Great Wall of China among Seven New World Wonders." Accessed July 19, 2007. www.newsgd.com/culture/culturenews/content/2007-07/09/content_4203263.htm.

People's Daily Online. "Regulation in Place to Preserve the Great Wall." June 27, 2003. english.peopledaily.com.cn/200306/27/eng20030627_118994.shtml.

Power, Matthew. "Hiking the Great Wall: Astride the Dragon's Back." National Geographic, July 9, 2008. www.nationalgeographic.com/adventure/0510/features/hiking_great_wall.html.

TravelChinaGuide.com. "Great Wall of China." Accessed July 23, 2007. www.travelchinaguide.com/china_great_wall/.

| | | | |

➤ Top Five Ancient Chinese Inventions

Columbia University. "Chinese Inventions: Can You Name Them?" *China: A Teaching Workbook*. Accessed February 27, 2009. afe.easia.columbia.edu/song/readings/inventions_ques.htm.

Embassy of the People's Republic of China in South Africa. "Four Great Inventions of Ancient China." December 13, 2004. www.chinese-embassy.org.za/eng/znjl/Culture/t174418.htm.

National High Magnetic Field Laboratory. "Early Chinese Compass." Accessed February 24, 2009. www.magnet.fsu.edu/education/tutorials/museum/chinesecompass.html.

National High Magnetic Field Laboratory. "Lodestone." Accessed February 24, 2009. www.magnet.fsu.edu/education/tutorials/museum/lodestone.html.

Pleskacheuskaya, Inesa. "The Centuries-Old Dream of Flight." *China Today*, August 2004.

Pravda.ru. "Pasta Was Invented by China, not Italy, Archaeologists Prove." October 12, 2005. Accessed March 9, 2009. english.pravda.ru/news/science/12-10-2005/68040-0/#.U5m4cig5uZE.

Roach, John. "4,000-Year-Old Noodles Found in China." National Geographic News. October 12, 2005. news.nationalgeographic.com/news/2005/10/1012_051012_chinese_noodles.html.

Robertson, Frank. *Triangle of Death: The Inside Story of the Triads—the Chinese Mafia*. London: Routledge, 1977.

Walter, Patrick. "The Chinese Probably Invented Alcohol." *Chemistry and Industry* (December 2004). www.highbeam.com/doc/1G1-126749790.html.

Wright, David Curtis. *The History of China*. Westport, CT: Greenwood Publishing Group, 2001.

| | | | |

➤ The Assassin's Creed: How Ninja Work

No sources.

| | | | |

➤ How Aborigines Work

Agence France-Presse. "$450,000 for 'Stolen' Aborigine." *New York Times*, August 2, 2007. www.nytimes.com/2007/08/02/world /asia/02australiabrfs.html?ex=1343793600&=7c73ab2fdaaacca 3&ei=5124&partner=permalink&exprod=permalink.

Agence France-Presse. "Australian Court Rules That the City of Perth Belongs to Aborigines." *New York Times*, September 21, 2006. www.nytimes.com/2006/09/21/world/asia/21australia.html ?_r=1&oref=slogin.

Australian Bureau of Statistics. "Aboriginal and Torres Strait Islander Population." Accessed January 21, 2008. www.abs.gov.au/aus stats/abs@.nsf/Lookup/2075.0main+features32011.

Australian Government—Culture and Recreation Portal. "Australian Indigenous Cultural Heritage." Accessed January 21, 2008. australia.gov.au/about-australia/australian-story/austn-indig enous-cultural-heritage.

Australian Human Rights and Equal Opportunity Commission. *Report of the National Inquiry into the Separation of Aboriginal and Torres Strait Islander Children from Their Families*. April 1997. Accessed January 21, 2008. www.humanrights.gov.au/publications /bringing-them-home-report-1997.

"Australian Parliament Expresses Regret for Injustice to Aborigines." *Jet Magazine*, September 13, 1999.

BBC News. "Australia Apology to Aborigines." January 30, 2008. news .bbc.co.uk/2/hi/asia-pacific/7216873.stm.

Bond, John. "Return to Cootamundra: Healing? For Me That's

Impossible, Val Linow Told John Bond." *For a Change*, December 2005. Accessed January 21, 2008. www.forachange .co.uk/browse/2084.html.

Dalmau, Tim. "Aboriginal Wisdom, Aboriginal Rights—Australian Aborigines." *Whole Earth Review* 74 (Spring 1992): 48-55.

Jacobs, Christine. "I Don't Want Your Pity, Just Listen." *For a Change*, August–September 2005. www.forachange.co.uk /browse/2060.html.

Marks, Kathy. "Aborigines Mark the Day They Became 'Humans.'" *The Independent*, May 26, 2007. able2know.org/topic/97052-1.

Marks, Kathy. "Cries of Racism over Plan to Cut Child Abuse in Aborigines." *The Independent*, June 29, 2007. news.independent .co.uk/world/australasia/article2720109.ece.

Marks, Kathy. "'Stolen Generation' Aborigine Wins Test Case." *Belfast Telegraph*, August 3, 2007.

Oppenheimer, Stephen. "Out of Africa." *The Independent*, July 9, 2003. www.independent.co.uk/news/science/out-of-africa-95400.html.

Parliament of Australia. "The Stolen Generation." October 22, 2009. Accessed January 21, 2008. australia.gov.au/about-australia /australian-story/sorry-day-stolen-generations.

Ravilious, Kate. "Aborigines, Europeans Share African Roots, DNA Suggests." National Geographic News. May 7, 2007. Accessed January 21, 2008. news.nationalgeographic.com/news /2007/05/070507-aborigines-dna.html.

Ross, Kate and John Taylor. "Improving Life Expectancy and Health Status: A Comparison of Indigenous Australians and New Zealand Maori." *Journal of Population Research* (September 2002): 219-238.

Suter, Keith. "Australia—One Land: Two Peoples." *The Contemporary Review* 283 (August 2003): 84.

Wade, Nicholas. "From DNA Analysis, Clues to a Single Australian

Migration." *New York Times*, May 8, 2007. Accessed January 21, 2008. www.nytimes.com/2007/05/08/science/08abor .html?scp=1&sq=Australian+Migration.

Zielinska, Edyta. "Walkabout." *Natural History* (September 2006).

| | | | |

"No One Expects the Spanish Inquisition!": How the Spanish Inquisition Worked

The Galileo Project. "The Inquisition." 1995. Accessed February 5, 2008. galileo.rice.edu/chr/inquisition.html.

Gui, Bernard. *The Inquisitor's Guide: A Medieval Manual on Heretics*. Edited by Janet Shirley. Welwyn Garden City, England: Ravenhall Books, 2006.

"Inquisition." *Catholic Encyclopedia*. 1910. Accessed February 5, 2008. www.newadvent.org/cathen/08026a.htm.

Kamen, Henry. *The Spanish Inquisition: A Historical Revision*. New Haven, CT: Yale University Press, 1999.

Lea, Henry Charles. *A History of the Inquisition of Spain*. New York: AMS Press, 1966.

McGill, Sara. *The Inquisition*. Toledo, OH: Great Neck Publishing, 2005.

Nickerson, Hoffman and Hilaire Belloc. *The Inquisition: A Political and Military Study of Its Establishment*. New York: Houghton Mifflin, 1932.

O'Brien, John A. *The Inquisition*. New York: Macmillan Publishing, 1973.

Olsen, Ted. "How the Inquisition Saved Lives." *Christian History & Biography* 83 (Summer 2004). www.ctlibrary.com/ch/2004 /issue83/5.07.html.

Pope John Paul II. "Address to Symposium on the Inquisition." La Santa Sede. October 31, 1998. www.vatican.va/holy_father /john_paul_ii/speeches/1998/october/documents/hf_jp-i i_spe_19981031_simposio_en.html.

Walsh, William Thomas. *Characters of the Inquisition*. New York: P.J. Kenedy and Sons, 1940.

Wicker, Benjamin D. "Status: Inquisition in the Catholic Church." *Lay Witness*, April 2000.

Zenit. "Balanced History of the Inquisition is Possible, Says Expert." June 16, 2004. Accessed February 5, 2008. www.zenit.org/article -10377?l=english.

| | | | |

➤ Five Medieval Torture Devices

Bachrach, Deborah. *The Inquisition*. San Diego: Lucent Books, 1995.

Beccaria, Cesare. *Of Crimes and Punishments*. Translated by Edward D. Ingraham. Philadelphia: Philip H. Nicklin, 1819.

Farrington, Karen. *History of Punishment and Torture*. London: Octopus Publishing Group, 2000.

Gallonio, Antonio. *Trattato Degli Instrumenti di Delle Varie Maniere di Martirizare (Tortures and Torments of the Christian Martyrs)*. Translated by A.R. Allinson. Paris: The Fortune Press, 1903.

Goldberg, Enid A. and Norman Itzkowitz. *Tomas de Torquemada: Architect of Torture during the Spanish Inquisition*. London: Franklin Watts, 2007.

Hunt, Lynn. *Inventing Human Rights*. New York: W.W. Norton and Company, 2007.

Innes, Brian. *The History of Torture*. New York: St. Martin's Press, 1998.

Kellaway, Jean. *The History of Torture and Execution*. London: Mercury Books, 2003.

Medieval Times & Castles. "The Breast Ripper." November 29, 2008. Accessed December 22, 2008. www.medievality.com/breast -ripper.html.

Medieval Times & Castles. "The Pear of Anguish." November 29, 2008. Accessed December 22, 2008. www.medievality.com/pear-of -anguish.html.

Parry, L.A. *The History of Torture in England*. Montclair, NJ: Patterson Smith, 1975.

| | | | |

➤ "All for One, One for All": How Musketeers Worked

BBC News. "Musketeers Carry Dumas to Pantheon." November 30, 2002. Accessed September 26, 2011. news.bbc.co.uk/2/hi/europe/2531617.stm.

Dumas, Alexandre. *The Three Musketeers*. Introduction by Marcel Girard. New York: Everyman's Library/E.P. Dutton, 1966.

FoodReference.com. "3 Musketeers Candy Bar." Accessed September 26, 2011. www.foodreference.com/html/f3musketeers.html.

Held, Robert. *The Age of Firearms*. New York: Harper & Brothers, 1957.

Internet Movie Database. "The Three Musketeers." Accessed September 26, 2011. www.imdb.com/title/tt1509767/.

Kelly, Jack. *Gunpowder: Alchemy, Bombards, and Pyrotechnics*. New York: Basic Books, 2004.

Nevill, Ralpg. "Musketeer History." The Swashbuckling Press. Accessed September 26, 2011. swashbucklingpress.webs.com/musketeerhistory.htm.

Rafferty, Terence. "All for One." *New York Times*, August 20, 2006. Accessed September 28, 2011. www.nytimes.com/2006/08/20/books/review/20pevear.html?pagewanted=all.

Scott, Richard Bodley. *Wars of Religion: Western Europe 1610–1660*. Oxford, England: Osprey Publishing, 2010.

| | | | |

➤ How Witchcraft Works

Bartel, Pauline. *Spellcasters: Witches and Witchcraft in History, Folklore, and Popular Culture*. Dallas: Taylor Trade Publishing, 2000.

Beliefnet.com. Accessed February 21, 2013. www.beliefnet.com/.

Cantrell, Gary. *Wiccan Beliefs & Practices*. St. Paul: Llewellyn Publications, 2001.

Covenant of the Goddess. Accessed February 21, 2013, www.cog.org/.

D'Amario, Alison. "FAQs about the Salem Witch Trials." 2012. Accessed January 18, 2008. Salem Witch Museum. www.salem witchmuseum.com/education/faq.shtml.

D'Amario, Alison. "The Salem Witch Trials of 1692." 2012. Accessed January 18, 2008. Salem Witch Museum. www.salemwitch museum.com/education/index.shtml.

Hoffer, Peter, PhD (professor of history, University of Georgia), personal interview with author, January 17, 2008.

Linder, Douglas. "The Witchcraft Trials in Salem: A Commentary." University of Missouri–Kansas City School of Law Faculty Project. March 2007. www.law.umkc.edu/faculty/projects /ftrials/salem/SAL_ACCT.HTM.

Marvel, Laura, ed. *The Salem Witch Trials*. San Diego: Greenhaven Press, 2003.

McCoy, Edain. *Spellworking for Covens: Magick for Two or More*. St. Paul: Llewellyn Publications, 2002.

RavenWolf, Silver. *To Stir a Magick Cauldron: A Witch's Guide to Casting and Conjuring*. St. Paul: Llewellyn Publications, 2001.

"The Reformation." *Catholic Encyclopedia*. Accessed February 21, 2013. www.newadvent.org/cathen/12700b.htm.

Salem, Massachusetts: The Comprehensive Salem Guide. "What about Witches." Accessed February 21, 2013. www.salemweb.com /guide/witches.shtml.

Shelton, Kisha. "Ergot: A History-Changing Plant Disease. Ergotism, Holy Fire, St. Anthony's Fire." University of Georgia, Plant Pathology Lab. September 5, 2001.

The Witches' League for Public Awareness. Accessed February 21, 2013. www.celticcrow.com/.

Witches' Voice Inc. Accessed February 21, 2013. www.witchvox.com/.

| | | | |

> **How Prohibition Worked**

"18: Prohibition." *Pittsburgh Post-Gazette*, November 27, 2002. www .post-gazette.com/nation/20021127amendment_18P9.asp.

Alcohol Alert. "2011 Drunk Driving Statistics." 2011. www.alcoholalert .com/drunk-driving-statistics.html.

Chicago Historical Society. "History Files: Al Capone." Accessed January 8, 2008. www.chicagohs.org/history/capone.html.

Digital History. "Jazz Age: The American 1920s." Accessed January 8, 2008. www.digitalhistory.uh.edu/era.cfm?eraID=13&smtID=2.

EyeWitness to History. "Prohibition." 2000. Accessed January 8, 2008. www.eyewitnesstohistory.com/snpmech2.htm.

Felix, Wanda. "The Trial of Fatty Arbuckle." Ralpmag.org. Accessed January 8, 2008. www.ralphmag.org/fatty.html.

Hanson, David J. "Dry Counties." Alcohol Problems and Solutions. Accessed December 9, 2007. www2.potsdam.edu/hansondj /Controversies/1140551076.html.

Library of Congress. "Prohibition in the Progressive Era." Accessed January 8, 2008. www.loc.gov/teachers/classroommaterials /presentationsandactivities/presentations/timeline/progress /prohib/.

PBS.org. "America 1900: Carrie Nation," *The American Experience*. Accessed January 8, 2008. www.pbs.org/wgbh/amex/1900 /peopleevents/pande4.html.

Rusty Cans. "'No Temperance in It': Woodrow Wilson & Prohibition." December 9, 2008. Accessed January 8, 2008. www.rustycans .com/HISTORY/prohibition.html.

Strasburger, Victor C. and Edward Donnerstein. "Children, Adolescents, and the Media: Issues and Solutions." *Pediatrics* 103 (January 1999): 129–139.

Tyrell, Ian. "Prohibition." American History for Australasian Schools.

Accessed December 9, 2007. www.anzasa.arts.usyd.edu.au/ahas
/prohibition_overview.html.

U.S. History. "Prohibition." Accessed January 8, 2008, www.u-s-history
.com/pages/h1085.html.

Women's Christian Temperance Union. Accessed January 8, 2008. www
.wctu.org/index.html.

| | | | |

➤ Top Five Marie Antoinette Scandals

"Affair of the Diamond Necklace." *Encyclopedia Britannica*. 2008. Accessed
August 1, 2008. www.britannica.com/EBchecked/topic/161488
/Affair-of-the-Diamond-Necklace.

Amiel, Barbara. "Misunderstood Marie Antoinette." *Maclean's* 119
(November 6, 2006): 48-50.

Baldrige, Letitia. *Taste: Acquiring What Money Can't Buy*. New York: St.
Martin's Press, 2007.

Covington, Richard. "Marie Antoinette." *Smithsonian*, November 2006.
Accessed August 1, 2008. www.smithsonianmag.com/history
/marie-antoinette-134629573/?no-ist.

Fraser, Antonia. *Marie Antoinette: The Journey*. New York: Anchor
Books, 2001.

The French Revolution. Directed by Doug Schultz. New York: A&E Home
Entertainment, 2005.

Goldberg, Jonah. "The Democrat's Frog Libel: Let Them Eat Cake
Economics." National Review Online. February 27, 2004.
Accessed August 1, 2008. www.nationalreview.com/articles
/209677/democrat-146-s-frog-libel.

Grubin, David. "'Let Them Eat Cake!' A New PBS Documentary
Examines the Many Myths Surrounding Marie Antoinette."
USA Today, September 2006.

"Hans Axel von Fersen." *Encyclopædia Britannica*. 2008. Accessed August 1,

2008. www.britannica.com/EBchecked/topic/205247/Hans
-Axel-von-Fersen.

Muschamp, Herbert. "A Current Affair." *New York Times Magazine*,
August 27, 2006. Accessed August 1, 2008. www.nytimes
.com/2006/08/27/style/tmagazine/t_w_1558_talk_icon_.html.

PBS. *Marie Antoinette and the French Revolution*. September 14, 2006.
Accessed August 1, 2008. www.pbs.org/marieantoinette/.

Schmidt, Carol. "She Never Said, 'Let Them Eat Cake.'" Montana State
University Research and Creative Activities. 2003. Accessed
August 1, 2008. www.montana.edu/wwwvr/activities/activities
04/Antoinette.html.

Street, Julie. "Long Live the Queen." *France Today*, June 1, 2008. Accessed
August 1, 2008. www.francetoday.com/articles/2008/06/01
/long-live-the-queen.html.

| | | | |

➤ Five of the Biggest Lies in History

Aron, Paul. *Mysteries in History: From Pre-History to the Present*. Santa
Barbara, CA: ABC-CLIO, 2005.

Danto, Arthur Coleman. *After the End of Art*. Princeton, NJ: Princeton
University Press, 1998.

Frullani, Anita. "The Piltdown Man Forgery." *British Heritage* 19 (April/
May 1998): 16.

Gernie, Sharif. *French Revolutions, 1815–1914*. Edinburgh: Edinburgh
University Press, 1999.

Haughton, Brian. *Hidden History*. Pompton Plains, NJ: Career Press, 2007.

Hoffer, Peter. *The Historian's Paradox*. New York: NYU Press, 2008.

Kidder, David and Noah D. Oppenheim. *The Intellectual Devotional:
American History*. Emmaus, PA: Rodale, 2007.

Landau, Ronnie S. *The Nazi Holocaust*. London: I.B. Tauris, 2006.

"Piltdown Man." *Encyclopaedia Britannica*. 2009. Accessed March 16, 2009. www.britannica.com/EBchecked/topic/460690/Piltdown-man.

Wilson, Colin. *The World's Greatest True Crime*. New York: Barnes & Noble Publishing, 2004.

| | | | |

➤ Five Impressive Art Heists

Associated Press. "$163 Million Art Heist in Zurich." CBS News. February 11, 2009. Accessed January 10, 2012. www.cbsnews.com/stories/2008/02/11/world/main3815033.shtml.

Associated Press. "2 Paintings Stolen From Zurich Museum Didn't Get Far." *New York Times*, February 20, 2008. Accessed January 10, 2012. www.nytimes.com/2008/02/20/world/europe/20zurich.html.

Associated Press. "Munch Masterpieces Join a Daunting List of Stolen Paintings." *USA Today*, August 23, 2004. Accessed January 21, 2012. www.usatoday.com/news/world/2004-08-23-stolen-paintings_x.htm.

Associated Press. "Solve Famed Boston Art Heist, Get $5M." CBS News. June 23, 2010. Accessed January 21, 2012. www.cbsnews.com/stories/2010/03/16/national/main6303926.shtml.

Bailey, Ronald. "The Monuments Men: Rescuing Art Plundered by Nazis." HistoryNet. April 19, 2007. Accessed January 12, 2012. www.historynet.com/the-monuments-men-rescuing-art-plundered-by-the-nazis.htm.

BBC News. "Greatest Art Heists in History." August 23, 2004. Accessed January 10, 2012. news.bbc.co.uk/1/hi/entertainment/arts/3590106.stm.

BBC News. "Scream Stolen from Norway Museum." August 22, 2004. Accessed January 11, 2012. news.bbc.co.uk/2/hi/europe/3588282.stm.

BBC News. "Stolen Rembrandt Work Recovered." September 16, 2005. Accessed January 8, 2012. news.bbc.co.uk/2/hi/entertainment/4252568.stm.

BBC News. "Stolen Renoir Recovered." April 6, 2001. Accessed January 9, 2012. news.bbc.co.uk/2/hi/entertainment/1263808.stm.

Bell, Rachael. "Sensational Art Heists from 'Mona Lisa' to Munch's 'The Scream.'" Crime Library. Accessed January 9, 2012. www.crimelibrary.com/gangsters_outlaws/outlaws/major_art_thefts/index.html.

Braver, Rita. "Rescuing Nazi-Looted Art." CBS News. January 27, 2008. Accessed January 9, 2012. www.cbsnews.com/stories/2008/01/27/sunday/main3755983.shtml.

Brooks, David. "Two Van Gogh Works Stolen from the Van Gogh Museum." Van Gogh Gallery. December 7, 2002. Accessed January 12, 2012. www.vggallery.com/news/20021207.htm.

FBI. "Art Crime Team." Accessed January 11, 2012. www.fbi.gov/about-us/investigate/vc_majorthefts/arttheft/art-crime-team.

FBI. "FBI Top Ten Art Crimes: Isabella Stewart Gardner Museum Theft." Accessed January 12, 2012. www.fbi.gov/about-us/investigate/vc_majorthefts/arttheft/isabella/.

Haq, Husna. "Paris Art Heist: The Chances of Recovery Aren't Good." *Christian Science Monitor*, May 20, 2010. Accessed January 10, 2012. www.csmonitor.com/USA/2010/0520/Paris-art-heist-The-chances-of-recovery-aren-t-good.

Harnischfeger, Uta. "Zurich Art Museum Robbed of a Cézanne, a Degas, a Van Gogh and a Monet." *International Herald Tribune*, February 11, 2008.

Iverson, Jeffrey T. "The French Art Heist: Who Would Steal Unsaleable Picassos?" *Time*, May 20, 2010. Accessed January 10, 2012. www.time.com/time/arts/article/0,8599,1990921,00.html.

Johnson, Kirk. "2 Are Convicted in Theft of Art at Warehouse." *New York Times*, April 11, 1987. Accessed January 21, 2012. www

.nytimes.com/1987/04/11/nyregion/2-are-convicted-in-theft
-of-art-at-warehouse.html.

Jones, Jonathan. "The Bigger Picture." *The Guardian*, February 16,
2007. Accessed January 21, 2012. www.guardian.co.uk/art
anddesign/2007/feb/17/art.arttheft.

Kurkjian, Stephen. "Secrets behind the Largest Art Heist in History." *The
Boston Globe*, March 13, 2005. Accessed January 9, 2012. www
.boston.com/news/specials/gardner_heist/heist/.

Lendon, Brad. "Reward Beats Risk for Art Thieves." CNN. February
14, 2008. Accessed January 13, 2012. www.cnn.com/2008
/CRIME/02/14/art.theft/index.html.

MacAskill, Ewen. "New Discovery Sheds Light on Nazi Art Theft."
The Guardian, November 1, 2007. Accessed January 10, 2012.
www.guardian.co.uk/world/2007/nov/01/usa.art.

NPR. "The Theft That Made the 'Mona Lisa' a Masterpiece." July 30,
2011. Accessed January 10, 2012. www.npr.org/2011/07/30
/138800110/the-theft-that-made-the-mona-lisa-a-masterpiece.

PBS. "Treasures of the World: Theft of the Mona Lisa." Accessed January
10, 2012. www.pbs.org/treasuresoftheworld/a_nav/mona_nav
/main_monafrm.html.

The Telegraph. "Art Theft: Some of the Famous Art Heists of the Past
100 Years." Accessed January. 11, 2012. www.telegraph.co.uk
/culture/culturepicturegalleries/8702071/Art-theft-some-of
-the-famous-art-heists-of-the-last-100-years.html?image=1.

Townsend, Mark and Caroline Davies. "Henry Moore Case Solved."
The Guardian, May 16, 2009. Accessed January 9, 2012. www
.guardian.co.uk/artanddesign/2009/may/17/henry-moore
-sculpture-theft-reclining-figure.

➤ Ten Terribly Bungled Crimes

Associated Press. "Bank Robber Uses Back of His Own Check to Write Stick-up Note." *Tucson Citizen*, September 12, 2007. tucsoncitizen.com/morgue/2007/09/12/62801-cops-bank -robber-uses-back-of-his-own-check-to-write-stick-up-note/.

Associated Press. "Bosnian Burglar Takes Nap, Gets Caught." *Boston Globe*, November 22, 2007.

Associated Press. "Brazil Arrests Alleged Leader of Gang in $70 Million Bank Robbery." *International Herald Tribune*, February 26, 2008.

Associated Press. "Goodfella's Guide to New York." CBS News. February 11, 2009. www.cbsnews.com/stories/2003/07/02/print/main 561401.shtml.

Associated Press. "Police: Mans Shoots Self in Groin during Robbery." MSNBC. January 16, 2008. www.msnbc.msn.com/id/22681900/.

Associated Press. "Woman Buys Fake Cocaine, Calls Cops to Help Her Get Refund." Fox News. August 13, 2007. www.foxnews .com/story/2007/08/13/woman-buys-fake-cocaine-calls-cops -to-help-her-get-refund/.

BBC News. "Grisly End for Unlucky Burglar." January 25, 2001. news .bbc.co.uk/1/hi/world/americas/1135660.stm.

CNN. "Five Guilty of 'Biggest Ever' UK Heist." January 28, 2008. www .cnn.com/2008/WORLD/europe/01/28/britain.heist/.

"Curiosity Catches a Fugitive." *Deseret Morning News*, October 16, 1988. nl.newsbank.com/nl-search/we/Archives?p_product=News Library&p_multi=DSNB&d_place=DSNB&p_theme=news library2&p_action=search&p_maxdocs=200&p_topdoc=1&p _text_direct-0=0F35F77CCBE3DB82&p_field_direct-0 =document_id&p_perpage=10&p_sort=YMD_date:D&s _trackval=GooglePM.

Easton, Adam. "Polish Author Jailed for Murder." BBC News. September 5, 2007. news.bbc.co.uk/2/hi/europe/6979457.stm.

Garner, Marcus K. "Ga. Bank Robber Nabbed While Waiting for

Getaway Bus." *Atlanta Journal-Constitution*, January 25, 2008. www.policeone.com/bizarre/articles/1654453/.

Goff, Liz. "Biggest Theft of Cash in History." *Queens Tribune*, December 11, 1978.

McGee, Scott. "Car Chase Ends, But Not Until after Suspect Stops for Cigs." 3TV. July 24, 2007.

Walker, Andrew. "How an Assassin Bungled a Deadly Umbrella Plot." *The Independent*, May 13, 2000.

WPLG. "Hungry Customer Displays Gun for Food." WPLG. www.local10.com/news/14320910/detail.html.

| | | | |

Did the Ancient Greeks Get Their Ideas from the Africans?

The Big View. "Thales." Accessed January 17, 2008. www.thebigview.com/greeks/thales.html.

Hooker, Richard. "Barbarians and Bureaucrats: Minoans, Myceneans, and the Greek Dark Ages." Washington State University, Learning Module. 1996. richard-hooker.com/sites/worldcultures/MINOA/MINOA.HTM.

Hooker, Richard. "Ma'at: Goddess of Truth; Truth and Order." Washington State University, Learning Module. 1996. richard-hooker.com/sites/worldcultures/EGYPT/MAAT.HTM.

McSwine, Bartley L. "The Role of Philosophy in the Breakdown of Modern Society Contrasted with the African Worldview and Intelligence in Ancient Kemet." *Journal of Philosophy and History of Education* 49 (1999): 147–151. www.journalofphilosophyandhistoryofeducation.com/jophe49.pdf.

Osler, William. "The Evolution of Modern Medicine." Lecture at Yale University, New Haven, CT, April 1913. emotional-literacy-education.com/classic-books-online-b/teomm10.htm.

Parrott, Annette M. "Timeline Comparing Science, Science Education and Technology Innovations and Developments." In J. Hassard, *The Art of Teaching Science*. New York: Oxford University Press, 2008.

Person-Lynn, Kwaku. "Afrikan Origins of the University." Exodus Online. February 11, 2005. www.exodusnews.com/HISTORY /History019.htm.

University of Alabama-Birmingham. "Formative and Classic Kemet: 31st to 16th c. B.C." Accessed January 17, 2008. www.hp.uab.edu /image_archive/um/umd.html.

Van Sertima, Ivan. *Egypt Revisited*. Livingston, NJ: Transaction Publishers, 1989.

| | | | | |

Was There Really a Curse on King Tutankhamen's Tomb?

Ceram, C.W. *Gods, Graves, and Scholars*. New York: Alfred A. Knopf, 1968.

Handwerk, Brian. "Egypt's 'King Tut Curse' Caused by Tomb Toxins?" National Geographic News. May 6, 2005. news.nationalgeo graphic.com/news/2005/05/0506_050506_mummycurse.html.

Lawler, Andrew. "A Mystery Fit for a Pharaoh." *Smithsonian Magazine*, July 2006.

Nelson, Mark R. "The Mummy's Curse: Historical Cohort Study." *British Medical Journal* 325 (December 21, 2002): 1482.

"Tutankhamen." *Encyclopædia Britannica*. July 10, 2013. Accessed June 12, 2014. www.britannica.com/EBchecked/topic/610635/Tutankhamen.

Wilford, John Noble. "Long Skull, Narrow Face: Tut Gets New Look." *New York Times*, May 11, 2005. www.nytimes.com/2005/05/11 /science/11tut.html?scp=14&sq=king+tut&st=nyt.

Wilford, John Noble. "Malaria Is a Likely Killer in King Tut's Post-

Mortem." *New York Times*, February 16, 2010. www.nytimes
.com/2010/02/17/science/17tut.html.

Wilford, John Noble. "World Briefing: Middle East: Egypt: A Tut
Mystery is Solved." *New York Times*, March 9, 2005. query.
nytimes.com/gst/fullpage.html?res=9E07E7DD163CF93AA
35750C0A9639C8B63&scp=17&sq=king+tut&st=nyt.

| | | | |

➤ Did the Dutch Really Trade Manhattan for Nutmeg?

Axelrod, Alan. *The Complete Idiot's Guide to American History*. New York:
Alpha Books, 2003.

"Banda Islands." *Encyclopedia Britannica*. 2009. Accessed April 20, 2009,
www.britannica.com/EBchecked/topic/51452/Banda-Islands.

Bernstein, William J. *A Splendid Exchange: How Trade Shaped the World*.
New York: Atlantic Monthly Press, 2008.

Carlisle, Rodney P. and J. Geoffrey Golson. *Colonial America from Settlement to
the Revolution*. Santa Barbara, CA: ABC-CLIO, 2006.

"Hudson, Henry." *Encyclopædia Britannica*. January 6, 2014. Accessed June
12, 2014. www.britannica.com/EBchecked/topic/274681
/Henry-Hudson.

Lamoureux, Florence. *Indonesia*. Santa Barbara, CA: ABC-CLIO, 2003.

Le Couteur, Penny and Jay Burreson. *Napoleon's Buttons: How 17 Molecules
Changed History*. New York: Penguin Group (USA), 2004.

McVeigh, Frank J. *Brief History of Social Problems: A Critical Thinking
Approach*. Lanham, MD: University Press of America, 2004.

Weir, Stephen. *History's Worst Decisions: And the People who Made Them*.
St. Leonards, Australia: Murdoch Books, 2005.

| | | | |

➤ Could Jack the Ripper Have Been an Artist?

Curtis, Lewis Perry. *Jack the Ripper and the London Press*. New Haven, CT: Yale University Press, 2001.

Dunn, Adam. "Patricia Cornwell vs. Jack the Ripper," CNN. December 3, 2002. archives.cnn.com/2002/SHOWBIZ/books/12/03/cornwell.ripper/index.html.

Gibbons, Fiachra. "Does this Painting by Walter Sickert Reveal the Identity of Jack the Ripper?" *The Guardian*, December 8, 2001. books.guardian.co.uk/news/articles/0,,615448,00.html.

McCrary, Gregg. "A Succession of Murders." The Crime Library. Accessed April 28, 2008. www.crimelibrary.com/serial_killers/notorious/ripper_profile/1_index.html.

"Novelist says British Artist May Have Been Jack the Ripper." *St. Petersburg Times*, October 31, 2002. www.sptimes.com/2002/10/31/Artsandentertainment/In_the_news.shtml.

Ryder, Stephen P. "Patricia Cornwell and Walter Sickert: A Primer." Casebook: Jack the Ripper. Accessed April 28, 2008. www.casebook.org/dissertations/dst-pamandsickert.html.

Vanderlinden, Wolf. "The Art of Murder." Ripper Notes. February 2002. www.casebook.org/dissertations/dst-artofmurder.html.

Willing, Richard. "Cornwell Paints 'Portrait' of Jack the Ripper." *USA Today*, November 18, 2002. www.usatoday.com/life/books/reviews/2002-11-18-cornwell-portrait_x.htm.

| | | | |

➤ Who Was Rosie the Riveter?

Kimble, James J. and Lester C. Olson. "Visual Rhetoric Representing Rosie the Riveter: Myth and Misconception in J. Howard Miller's 'We Can Do It!' Poster." *Rhetoric and Public Affairs* 9 (2006): 533–569.

National Park Service. "Rosie the Riveter: Women Working during

World War II." Accessed October 27, 2008. www.nps.gov /pwro/collection/website/rosie.htm.

National Park Service. "Rosie the Riveter World War II Home Front." July 14, 2008. Accessed October 27, 2008. www.nps.gov/rori /index.htm.

PBS. "Betty Freidan and *The Feminine Mystique.*" *The First Measured Century*, Program Segments 1960–2000. Accessed October 27, 2008. www.pbs.org/fmc/segments/progseg11.htm.

PBS. "The Perilous Fight: Women." *America's World War II in Color*, 2003. Accessed October 27, 2008. www.pbs.org/perilousfight /social/women/.

PBS. "World War II: The Homefront." *The First Measured Century*, Program Segments 1930–1960. Accessed October 27, 2008. www.pbs.org/fmc/segments/progseg8.htm.

Rosie the Riveter Trust. "Rosie the Riveter." Accessed October 27, 2008. www.rosietheriveter.org/.

U.S. Department of Transportation, Federal Highway Administration. "Women in Transportation: Rosie the Riveter." December 3, 1999. Accessed October 27, 2008. www.fhwa.dot.gov/wit /rosie.htm.

| | | | | |

➤ Did the CIA Test LSD on Unsuspecting Americans?

Baker, Russell. "Acid, Americans, and the Agency." *The Guardian*, February 14, 1999. www.guardian.co.uk/Archive/Article/0,4273,3821 747,00.html.

Budiansky, Stephen, Erica Goode, and Ted Gest. "The Cold War Experiments." *U.S. News and World Report*, January 24, 1994.

Davenport-Hines, Richard. *The Pursuit of Oblivion: A Global History of Narcotics.* New York: W.W. Norton & Company, 2004.

The Science Channel. "Inside Mind Control." Accessed September 17, 2008. science.discovery.com/stories/mkultra.html.

Stratton, Richard. "Altered States of America." *SPIN Magazine*, March 1994. www.frankolsonproject.org/Articles/Spin.html.

Turner, Admiral Stansfield. "Prepared Statement of CIA Director Stansfield Turner." U.S. Senate, August 3, 1977. www.druglibrary.org /schaffer/history/e1950/mkultra/Hearing02.htm.

U.S. Senate. "Project MKULTRA, the CIA's Program of Research into Behavior Modification." August 3, 1977. www.druglibrary.org /schaffer/history/e1950/mkultra/Hearing01.htm.

U.S. Senate. "Testing and Use of Chemical and Biological Agents by the Intelligence Community." August 3, 1977. www.druglibrary .org/schaffer/history/e1950/mkultra/AppendixA.htm.

Valentine, Douglas. "Sex, Drugs, and the CIA." CounterPunch. June 20, 2002. www.counterpunch.org/valentine0621.html.

Contributors

Josh Clark

Matt Cunningham

Shanna Freeman

Ed Grabianowski

Alia Hoyt

Ryan Johnson

Candace Keener

John Kelley

Julia Layton

Jane McGrath

Lee Ann Obringer

About HowStuffWorks

For years, the hosts of *Stuff You Missed in History Class*, the immensely popular podcast from the website HowStuffWorks.com, have been giving listeners front row seats to some of the most astonishing and amazing tales the human record has to offer. Now, more than one hundred million downloads later, they've carefully compiled this book from some of the best content on HowStuffWorks.com. It gives readers the chance to hide in the shadow of the ninja, brandish a blade like the best musketeer, or plunder a monastery alongside the impossibly fierce Vikings. Come along for the adventure and stay for the education. You haven't met history like this before.

HowStuffWorks.com is an award-winning digital source of credible, unbiased, and easy-to-understand explanations of how the world actually works. Founded in 1998, the site is now an online resource for millions of people of all ages. From car engines to search engines, from cell phones to stem cells, and thousands of subjects in between, HowStuffWorks.com has it covered. In addition to comprehensive articles, our helpful graphics and informative videos walk you through every topic clearly and objectively. Our premise is simple: demystify the world and do it in a clear-cut way that anyone can understand.

If you enjoyed *Stuff You Missed in History Class*, check out the rest of the series from Sourcebooks and HowStuffWorks.com!

THE REAL SCIENCE OF SEX APPEAL: WHY WE LOVE, LUST, AND LONG FOR EACH OTHER

EVER WONDER WHY LOVE MAKES US SO CRAZY? COME DIVE INTO THE *REAL* SCIENCE BEHIND SEX APPEAL AND WHY WE LOVE, LUST, AND LONG FOR EACH OTHER.

Did you know your walk, your scent, and even the food you eat can make you sexier? Or that there are scientifically proven ways to become more successful at dating, especially online? The team at the award-winning website HowStuffWorks reveals the steamy science of love and sex, from flirting to falling in love and everything in between. Discover:

➤ How aphrodisiacs and sex appeal work (and how to increase yours!)

➤ Whether love at first sight is scientifically possible

➤ Why breakup songs hurt so good

➤ What happens in the brain during an orgasm

➤ The crazy chemistry behind long-term relationships

➤ The dope on dating and matchmaking

➤ And much more!

This dynamic book will show you what to expect—and what to do—the next time someone sets your heart racing.

THE SCIENCE OF SUPERHEROES AND SPACE WARRIORS: LIGHTSABERS, BATMOBILES, KRYPTONITE, AND MORE!

DO YOU HAVE WHAT IT TAKES TO BE A SUPERHERO?

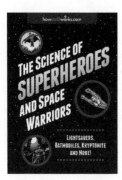

You picked out your superpower years ago. You can change into your costume in seconds. You could take out a Sith Lord with your lightning-quick lightsaber moves. Not so fast! Before you can start vanquishing bad guys, it's important to be schooled in the science of saving the world. Come learn the science behind your favorite superheroes and supervillains and their ultracool devices and weapons—from Batmobiles and warp speed to lightsabers, Death Stars, and kryptonite—and explore other cool technologies from the science fiction realm in this dynamic book. Discover:

➤ How Batman and the Batmobile really work

➤ 10 *Star Trek* technologies that actually came true

➤ Whether warp speed and lightsabers are really possible

➤ If Superman would win against Harry Potter, Sith Lords, and even Chuck Norris!

➤ How new liquid body armor can make us superhuman

➤ And more!

Prepare to do battle with the world's most evil masterminds!

FUTURE TECH, RIGHT NOW: X-RAY VISION, MIND CONTROL, AND OTHER AMAZING STUFF FROM TOMORROW

FROM X-RAY VISION TO MIND READING, THE FUTURE IS COMING ON FAST!

Flying Cars! Teleporting! Robot servants! Wouldn't you love any of these? You're in luck because they may be closer to reality than you think. Based on the best of HowStuffWorks' popular podcasts TechStuff and Stuff to Blow Your Mind, this dynamic book reveals the science of our future, from mind control and drugs that can make you smarter to textbooks that talk to you and even robotic teammates. Discover:

➤ How telekinesis and digital immortality work

➤ Whether computers could replace doctors one day

➤ What robot servants and coworkers will look like

➤ Five of the coolest future car technologies

➤ What we will do for fun in 2050

➤ And much more!

Come explore the coolest and craziest technology of the future.